OSAMA BIN LADEN
DEAD OR ALIVE?

DATE DUE

David Ray Griffin's previous book, The New Pearl Harbor Revisited, *received an honor that is bestowed on only 51 books a year. On November 24, 2008, this book was named "Pick of the Week" by* Publishers Weekly, *a prestigious publication that has guided booksellers, librarians, literary agents, and publishers for over 100 years.*

ADVANCE PRAISE FOR *OSAMA BIN LADEN: DEAD OR ALIVE?*

"David Ray Griffin, one of America's most careful and judicious political analysts, specializes in subjects the mainstream media and most politicians prefer to ignore. Three cheers to him now for taking on the question of whether Osama bin Laden died some years ago and should therefore no longer be a reason for the United States to continue its war in Afghanistan. There are powerful forces both in the United States and some of its allies that undoubtedly want a clash of civilizations. Some of these forces may well have acted secretly in the past, and may still be working, to create situations, real or false, to bring about more warfare. Griffin's new book, with its evidence that 'messages from bin Laden' may have been fabricated, should encourage a complete rethinking of the mission in Afghanistan."

—William Christison, former senior CIA official

"Osama bin Laden is the world's best-known terrorist, but how much of what we think we know about him is real? David Griffin examines this question in greater depth than any previous author. Based on the evidence, he suggests that bin Laden may have been dead for some time. If so, this means that some covert operators have been fabricating tapes to keep Osama bin Laden alive in the public's imagination."

—Terrell E. Arnold, former deputy director of the US State Department Office of Counterterrorism, author of *A World Less Safe*

"This book is part of a growing body of nonfiction that illuminates the cataclysmic gap between those with power, who do as they please, and those with knowledge, who are not heard. ... President Obama [must] break out of the closed circle of power to connect with the kind of independent knowledge found in this book..."

—Robert David Steele Vivas, recovering spy, founder of the USMC Intelligence Center, CEO of OSS.Net, and CEO of Earth Intelligence Network

OSAMA BIN LADEN
DEAD OR ALIVE?

DAVID RAY GRIFFIN

OLIVE
BRANCH
PRESS

An imprint of Interlink Publishing Group, Inc.
www.interlinkbooks.com

3 1218 00434 2243

First published in 2009 by

OLIVE BRANCH PRESS
An imprint of Interlink Publishing Group, Inc.
46 Crosby Street, Northampton, Massachusetts 01060
www.interlinkbooks.com

Copyright © David Ray Griffin 2009

Library of Congress Cataloging-in-Publication Data
Griffin, David Ray, 1939–
Osama Bin Laden : dead or alive? / by David Ray Griffin.
p. cm.
Includes bibliographical references and index.
ISBN 978-1-56656-783-1 (pbk.)
1. Bin Laden, Osama, 1957– 2. War on Terrorism, 2001- 3. Middle East—Foreign relations—
United States. 4. United States—Foreign relations—Middle East. I. Title.
HV6432.G75 2009
363.325092—dc22

200901277

Cover: The image taken from a video released by Qatar's Al-Jazeera televison broadcast on Friday, October 5, 2001, is said to show Osama bin Laden at an undisclosed location. Al-Jazeera did not say whether the image was taken before or after the September 11 attacks on the United States or how they obtained it. Bin Laden is believed to have been at a celebration of the union of his al-Qaida network and al-Zawahri's Egyptian Jihad group.
© AP Photo/Courtesy of Al-Jazeera via APTN

Printed and bound in the United States of America

To request our 40-page full-color catalog, please visit our website at: www.interlinkbooks.com, call us toll-free at: 1-800-238-LINK, or write to us at: Interlink Publishing, 46 Crosby Street, Northampton, MA 01060

Contents

ACKNOWLEDGMENTS

I wish to express my gratitude to Matthew Everett, Tod Fletcher, and Elizabeth Woodworth, all of whom gave me great assistance in the preparation of this little book. I am also grateful to Michel Moushabeck and Pamela Thompson, the publisher and editor of Olive Branch Press, respectively, for getting this book out quickly, and to Hilary Plum, who took care of the actual editing, so that it might make a contribution to the discussion of what the Obama administration should do about the war in Afghanistan. Special thanks, finally, are owed to Robert Baer, who not only read the essay but also allowed me to quote a statement he made in response.

INTRODUCTION

On October 2, 2008, former CIA operative Robert Baer—who wrote the book that inspired the film *Syriana*[1]—was interviewed on National Public Radio's *Fresh Air*. Near the end of the interview, Baer expressed his opinion in passing that Osama bin Laden was dead. Later, when the interviewer, Terry Gross, asked Baer about this, he said: "Of course he's dead." Baer elaborated:

> He hasn't shown up. I've taken in the last month a poll of CIA officers who have been on his trail, and what astounded me was not a single one was sure he was alive or dead. In other words, they have no idea. I mean, this man disappeared off the side of the earth. That has never happened before in my years in the CIA.[2]

The following month, on November 10, 2008, the National Terror Alert Response Center said that Osama bin Laden was reportedly planning a new attack on the United States that "will 'outdo by far' the attacks of September 11 in 2001."[3] This alert was derived from a story in a London-based Arabic newspaper, which stated that this information came from a Yemeni official who, although "not named," was said to be "very close to Al-Qaeda." The alert also passed on the story's claim that "only six months ago, bin Laden sent a message to all jihad cells in the Arab world."[4] Accordingly, the alert, like the story on which it was based, was written as if there were no question about the continued existence of Osama bin Laden.

The next day, November 11, 2008, a *Washington Post* story said:

> President-elect Barack Obama... intends to renew the US commitment to the hunt for Osama bin Laden.... "This is our enemy," one adviser said of bin Laden, "and he should be our principal target."... [Obama's] national security transition teams... have not yet plotted their diplomatic approach to Pakistan, where US intelligence officials believe bin Laden is hiding."[5]

The *Post*'s story did not mention that some US intelligence officials believe that bin Laden is not hiding *anywhere*—because he is dead.

The view that he is dead is, moreover, not held only by Robert Baer and some of his friends in the CIA. In March 2009, Angelo Codevilla, a former Foreign Service officer who now teaches international relations at Boston University and serves as a senior editor of the *American Spectator*, published an article in that magazine titled "Osama bin Elvis." Explaining this title, he wrote: "Seven years after Osama bin Laden's last verifiable appearance among the living, there is more evidence for Elvis's presence among us than for his."[6]

Obviously, if bin Laden is dead, a hunt to find him would necessarily be futile. To have a rational policy, therefore, the Obama administration will first need to determine whether bin Laden is dead or alive.

There is evidence on both sides of this question. The main evidence that he is dead comes from reports that he died in Tora Bora late in 2001, combined with the fact that communications with him had been regularly intercepted until then and those interceptions came to an end at that time. The main evidence that bin Laden is still alive comes from messages, purportedly from him, that are contained in audio- and videotapes. Obviously, if bin Laden has been dead since late 2001, all of these messages have been fabricated. But if at least some of them are authentic, then the reports of his death in 2001 were untrue.

The question, accordingly, is whether the reasons to consider at least some of these messages authentic are strong enough to outweigh the evidence that Osama bin Laden has long been dead. In this book's first chapter, I look at evidence for his early death. I then turn, in the later chapters, to the question of the authenticity of the "Osama bin Laden videos" and other alleged communications from him.

1

EVIDENCE THAT OSAMA BIN LADEN IS DEAD

In this chapter, I look at various types of evidence that Osama bin Laden is dead. For the most part, I deal with this evidence chronologically, beginning with reports that a funeral for him occurred on or about December 15, 2001.

BIN LADEN FUNERAL REPORTS

On December 26, 2001, an article entitled "News of Bin Laden's Death and Funeral 10 Days Ago" appeared in the Egyptian newspaper *Al-Wafd*. Based on a story in Pakistan's *Observer* that was published on December 25, it said:

> Islamabad: A prominent official in the Afghan Taleban movement announced yesterday the death of Osama bin Laden, the chief of al-Qa'da organization, stating that bin Laden suffered serious complications in the lungs and died a natural and quiet death. The official, who asked to remain anonymous, stated to *The Observer* of Pakistan that he had himself attended the funeral of bin Laden and saw his face prior to burial in Tora Bora 10 days ago. He mentioned that 30 of al-Qa'da fighters attended the burial as well as members of his family and some friends from the Taleban. In the farewell ceremony to his final rest guns were fired in the air. The official stated that it is difficult to pinpoint the burial location of bin Laden because according to the Wahhabi tradition no mark is left by the grave.[1]

According to this article, therefore, bin Laden's funeral took place ten days before December 25, 2001, which would have been December 15. Given the Muslim custom of burying the dead

— 1 —

quickly,[2] this would mean that he had probably died only a day or two earlier, hence December 13 or 14.

This report was publicized in the United States by Fox News, which on December 26 ran a story headed: "Report: Bin Laden Already Dead." Drawing directly from the original report published in Pakistan, Fox News said:

> Usama bin Laden has died a peaceful death due to an untreated lung complication, the *Pakistan Observer* reported, citing a Taliban leader who allegedly attended the funeral of the Al Qaeda leader. … Bin Laden, according to the source, was suffering from a serious lung complication and succumbed to the disease in mid-December, in the vicinity of the Tora Bora mountains. The source claimed that bin Laden was laid to rest honorably in his last abode and his grave was made as per his Wahabi belief.… The Taliban source who claims to have seen bin Laden's face before burial said "he looked pale… but calm, relaxed and confident."[3]

Apparently, no one from bin Laden's inner circle issued a statement at the time contradicting this report.

WHITE HOUSE RESPONSE TO THE BIN LADEN VIDEO RELEASED DECEMBER 27, 2001

On December 27, 2001, a video purportedly from bin Laden was aired by Al-Jazeera television. Although the speaker did not take credit for the 9/11 attacks, he praised "the 19 students who shook the American empire." There seemed no doubt, based on the speaker's appearance,[4] that he truly was Osama bin Laden. Although an article in London's *Telegraph* said that the Bush administration "dismissed" the video, it dismissed only the bravado of the message—which called on Muslims to "concentrate on hitting the US economy with every available means [because] if their economy is finished they will become too busy to enslave oppressed people."[5]

The Osama bin Laden of this video appeared to be quite unwell, perhaps near death. According to the *Telegraph* article, the speaker had a "gaunt, frail appearance," his "beard was much whiter than on November 3, the last time al Jazeera broadcast a video of [bin Laden], and he appeared much older than his 44 years." Also noteworthy was "bin Laden's left arm, which hung limply by his side while he gesticulated with his right."

The Bush administration suggested, in fact, that the release of the video at that time could mean that bin Laden was dead. According to one White House aide, "[bin Laden] could have made the video and then ordered that it be released in the event of his death."[6]

This suggestion, besides probably being inspired partly by the story about bin Laden's funeral (although the *Telegraph* article did not mention it), was also based on a report that, although bin Laden's voice had been "detected regularly until two weeks ago [this would have been two weeks before December 27, hence about December 13] by intelligence operatives monitoring radio transmissions in Tora Bora," it had not been heard since, and "President Bush [had] hinted in private that bin Laden's silence could mean he has been killed."[7] At that time, therefore, it appears that the Bush White House believed that bin Laden was possibly dead.

As to when this video was made, all we know for sure is that, besides being made *before* December 27 (when it was aired by Al-Jazeera), it was made *after* November 16, because in it bin Laden referred to the bombing of the mosque at Khost, which took place on November 16, as having occurred "a few days ago."[8] Besides referring to it as the "video released December 27," therefore, we can also call it the "post–November 16 video."

SECRETARY OF DEFENSE RUMSFELD AND COALITION LEADER KENTON KEITH

President Bush and the White House aide quoted in the *Telegraph* article were not the only persons in the Bush administration to suggest that bin Laden might be dead. The *Telegraph* article also quoted Secretary of Defense Donald Rumsfeld as saying, in response to a report about bin Laden's whereabouts: "We do know of certainty that he is in Afghanistan or some other country or dead."[9]

Having gotten a laugh from this line, Rumsfeld would use it again a few months later while speaking to troops in Kyrgyzstan, saying:

> We're hunting [bin Laden] down, we're tracking him down, he's hiding. We haven't heard hide nor hair of him since, oh, about December, in terms of anything hard. We don't know where he is. We are pretty sure he is either dead or alive.[10]

It would appear, therefore, that for at least the early months of 2002, Rumsfeld was seriously entertaining the idea that bin Laden was dead.

Still another US official, Kenton Keith, the spokesman for the US-led coalition in Afghanistan, expressed this possibility, saying on December 24, 2001, that "bin Laden might have been killed in intense US bombings of his Tora Bora cave-complex."[11]

PAKISTAN'S PRESIDENT MUSHARRAF AND A BUSH ADMINISTRATION OFFICIAL

The previous day, moreover, the same thought had been expressed by a US ally, Pakistan's President Pervez Musharraf, who spoke of the possibility of "bin Laden having died in U.S. airstrikes."[12]

Less than a month later, on January 19, 2002, Musharraf again suggested that bin Laden was dead, although this time he gave a different cause, telling CNN: "I think now, frankly, he is dead for the reason he is a... kidney patient." According to the resulting CNN story, headlined "Musharraf: Bin Laden Likely Dead," the Pakistani president said that bin Laden had taken two dialysis machines into Afghanistan, one of which was for his personal use. He then added: "[T]he photographs that have been shown of him on television show him extremely weak. ... I would give the first priority that he is dead."[13]

CNN then quoted a senior Bush administration official as saying that, although this was simply "a guess" on Musharraf's part, "it is a decent and reasonable conclusion—a good guess." This official further stated that, according to US intelligence, bin Laden needed dialysis every three days, adding: "[I]t is fairly obvious that that could be an issue when you are running from place to place,and facing the idea of needing to generate electricity in a mountain."[14]

CNN AND DR. SANJAY GUPTA

Two days later, on January 21, 2002, CNN followed up this report with a segment in which Paula Zahn interviewed Dr. Sanjay Gupta, CNN's medical correspondent. The focus was on bin Laden's appearance in the post–November 16 video, which had been released December 27, in which he had a "gaunt, frail appearance," whiter hair than before, and a limp left arm.

Contrasting the bin Laden of this video with pictures taken months earlier, Gupta referred to "a frosting over of his features— his sort of grayness of beard, his paleness of skin, very gaunt sort of features," which, he said, suggested "chronic illness." Getting more specific, Gupta added:

> The sort of frosting of the appearance is something that people a lot of times associate with chronic kidney failure, renal failure, certainly someone who is requiring dialysis would have that. He's also not moving his arms. I looked at this tape all the way through its entire length. He never moved his left arm at all. The reason that might be important is because people who have had a stroke— and certainly people are at increased risk of stroke if they also have kidney failure—he may have had a stroke and therefore is not moving his left side.

Paula Zahn then made a reference to Musharraf's report that bin Laden had imported two dialysis machines into Afghanistan, to which Gupta responded:

> [R]enal dialysis—talking about hemodialysis—is something that really is reserved for patients in end-stage renal failure. That means their kidneys have just completely shut down. The most common cause of something like that would be something like diabetes and hypertension.

Gupta then added:

> [I]ncidentally, dialysis machines require electricity,
> they're going to require clean water, they're going to
> require a sterile setting—infection is a huge risk with
> that. If you don't have all those things and a functioning
> dialysis machine, it's unlikely that you'd survive beyond
> several days or a week at the most.

Finally, in response to Zahn's next question—if bin Laden had
everything necessary to keep the machine running, how much help
would he need to administer the treatment?—Gupta replied:

> You certainly need someone who really knows how to run
> that dialysis machine. You have to have someone who's
> actually assessing his blood, Osama bin Laden's blood, to
> see what particular dialysate he would need, and to be able
> to change his dialysate as needed. So you'd need a kidney
> specialist, a technician—quite a few people around him.[15]

Gupta's statements in this interview gave an additional reason to
suspect that Osama bin Laden had died shortly after the post–
November 16 video had been made.

CNN AND PETER BERGEN

On February 1, 2002, CNN's Paula Zahn again discussed bin
Laden's health, this time with Peter Bergen, an expert on terrorism
in general and Osama bin Laden in particular. The focus was on an
interview with bin Laden that had been videotaped by Al-Jazeera in
late October 2001, parts of which had been aired by CNN on
January 31, 2002. When Zahn asked Bergen to compare the man
in this video with the Osama bin Laden he had interviewed in 1997,
Bergen replied: "He's actually quite similar. I mean, in terms of his
demeanor and his voice…. The big difference is that he's aged enormously between '97 and October of last year."

Turning then to the post–November 16 video (which had been
released December 27, 2001), Bergen made comments about it
similar to those previously made by Dr. Sanjay Gupta, saying:

> This is a man who was clearly not well. I mean, as you
> see from these pictures here, he's really, by December he's
> looking pretty terrible. But by December, of course, that
> tape that was aired then, he's barely moving the left side
> of his body. So he's clearly got diabetes.... He's appar-
> ently got dialysis... for kidney problems.

Zahn closed the interview by saying: "And, of course, the question
that people continue to debate is not only is he not well, is he still
alive today?"[16]

EARLIER EVIDENCE OF BIN LADEN'S KIDNEY DISEASE

Osama bin Laden's need for dialysis had been reported even before
Musharraf mentioned it in January 2002. On October 31, 2001, a
leading Parisian newspaper, *Le Figaro*, published a story reporting,
among other things, that bin Laden had been treated in the urology
department of the American Hospital in Dubai in July 2001 and
had ordered a mobile dialysis machine to be delivered to
Afghanistan.[17] Labeviere's story was reported that same day
(October 31) by United Press International.[18] It was further publicized in the English-speaking world the following day by
well-known British author Anthony Sampson in the *Guardian*[19] and
also by a story in the *Times* of London entitled "Ailing bin Laden
'Treated for Kidney Disease.'"[20] Reports a few months later that bin
Laden had died should, therefore, have been no surprise.

Time MAGAZINE

The possibility that bin Laden might be dead was further publicized
to the American people in the June 23, 2002, issue of *Time* magazine, which had a story entitled "Osama bin Laden: Dead or Alive?"
It began:

> The last time the world heard from Osama bin Laden,
> there was reason to believe his end was near. In a video-
> tape released in December, bin Laden looked sallow; his
> speech was slow, and his left arm immobile.

Citing Pentagon officials who admitted that bin Laden had "gone missing," this story added:

> Missing, of course, could mean dead, and a small minority of officials in the Pentagon, CIA and FBI believe that bin Laden's public silence since the December tape suggests he has succumbed—if not to U.S. air strikes, then possibly to kidney failure.

This *Time* story did lean toward what it reported to be the White House's view—that bin Laden was "still alive" but was "just being really quiet." The story, however, added that the White House could not say for certain one way or the other. Elaborating on the point about bin Laden's silence, the writer said:

> In the past, the U.S. has tried to nail bin Laden by tracking him electronically, using surveillance drones to listen to his communications and then drop a bomb fast. But military and intelligence sources say that since December his signal has gone dead.

"[T]he fact is," the writer concluded from this silence, "Washington just doesn't know."[21]

FBI COUNTERTERRORISM CHIEF DALE WATSON

The following month, one of the FBI officials who believed bin Laden to be dead spoke out publicly. In a July 17, 2002, story headed "FBI Official Thinks Bin Laden Is Dead," CBS News quoted Dale Watson, "the top official for counterterrorism and counterintelligence in the FBI," as saying: "I personally think [bin Laden] is probably not with us anymore." Although Watson added that he had "no evidence to support that [belief]," CBS provided some, saying:

> Adding to the speculation [about bin Laden's demise] is the fact that it's been several months since bin Laden has been seen, and with each taped appearance his health and appearance seemed to deteriorate.[22]

AMIR TAHERI IN THE *New York Times*

On July 11, 2002—about a week before the CBS News story on Dale Watson appeared—the *New York Times* carried an article by Amir Taheri, the editor of a Paris-based journal, *Politique Internationale*. Expressing his view that bin Laden was dead even more strongly than would Watson, Taheri began his article thus:

> Osama bin Laden is dead. The news first came from sources in Afghanistan and Pakistan almost six months ago: the fugitive died in December and was buried in the mountains of southeast Afghanistan. Pakistan's president, Pervez Musharraf, echoed the information.

Then, providing an additional reason to infer from bin Laden's recent silence that he had died, Taheri added:

> With an ego the size of Mount Everest, Osama bin Laden would not have, could not have, remained silent for so long if he were still alive. He always liked to take credit even for things he had nothing to do with. Would he remain silent for nine months and not trumpet his own survival?

Taheri concluded by saying:

> Mr. bin Laden's ghost may linger on—perhaps because Washington and Islamabad will find it useful. President Bush's party has a crucial election to win and Pervez Musharraf is keen to keep Pakistan in the limelight as long as possible. But the truth is that Osama bin Laden is dead.[23]

It would seem that, by publishing this story, the *New York Times* considered this claim to be credible.

CNN: BIN LADEN'S BODYGUARDS NOT WITH HIM

That same month CNN provided still more support for this conclusion in a report by Kelli Arena and CNN's Pentagon correspondent, Barbara Starr. Headlined "Sources: No Bodyguards, No bin Laden," their report of July 30, 2002, began:

> Some members of Osama bin Laden's security detail have been captured and are among the detainees at Guantánamo Bay, Cuba, U.S. officials told CNN Tuesday. Sources believe that if the bodyguards were captured away from bin Laden, it is likely the most-wanted man in the world is dead. The sources said the guards have been in custody since February. The revelation is the latest circumstantial and anecdotal evidence suggesting the al Qaeda leader might have been killed in the U.S.-led military action to purge the Taliban from power in Afghanistan. Some high-level U.S. officials are already convinced by such evidence that bin Laden, who has not been seen or heard from in months, is dead.

Reminding us that the FBI's Dale Watson had supported this conclusion earlier that month, Arena and Starr cautioned that "there is not enough evidence to draw a firm conclusion about bin Laden's fate"—including not "anything to suggest he remains alive."[24]

OLIVER NORTH IN THE *New York Times*
The next month (August 2002), the *New York Times* provided further support for the conclusion that bin Laden was *not* alive. In an article about a novel written by Colonel Oliver North—known both for his role in the Iran–Contra scandal and his later work as a commentator on Fox News—reporter Philip Shenon concluded by discussing an idea suggested in the novel: that there had been a conspiracy between Osama bin Laden and Saddam Hussein. Having asked North whether he himself believed this, Shenon wrote:

> Mr. North said he doubted there was such a conspiracy. And certainly there is none now, he said, because he is convinced that Mr. bin Laden is dead, quite possibly buried beneath the rubble of an American airstrike in Afghanistan. "I'm certain that Osama is dead," Mr. North said.... "I'm convinced of it, absolutely. And so are all the other guys I stay in touch with."[25]

Shenon offered no rebuttal.

PRESIDENT HAMID KARZAI

In October 2002—the month after the first anniversary of the 9/11 attacks—additional support for the idea that bin Laden had long been dead came from three of America's allies, all of whom had especially good means for knowing the relevant evidence. One of these was Hamid Karzai, the president of Afghanistan. On October 7, 2002, CNN ran a segment headlined "Karzai: Bin Laden 'Probably' Dead," in which Karzai said:

> I would come to believe that [bin Laden] is probably dead. But still, you never know. He might be alive. Five months ago, six months ago, I was thinking that he was alive. The more we don't hear of him, and the more time passes, there is that likelihood that he probably is either dead or seriously wounded somewhere.[26]

ISRAELI INTELLIGENCE

Nine days later, on October 16, 2002, this likelihood was stated with even more confidence in a *World Tribune* article entitled "Israeli Intelligence: Bin Laden is Dead, Heir Has Been Chosen." Referring to sources within Israel's intelligence community, this article said:

> The Israeli sources said Israel and the United States assess that Bin Laden probably died in the U.S. military campaign in Afghanistan in December. They said the emergence of new messages by Bin Laden are probably fabrications…. The sources said Al Qaida has already determined Bin Laden's heir. They said the heir has not been identified, but is probably not Bin Laden's son, Saad.

Especially relevant to the present essay is the statement by these Israeli intelligence sources that "new messages by Bin Laden are probably fabrications."

This *World Tribune* article also expressed skepticism about a recent statement of support for bin Laden's continued existence, saying:

> Earlier this week, Bin Laden's deputy, Ayman Zawahiri
> [*sic*], was said to have released a videotape in which he
> claims that the Al Qaida leader is alive and functioning.
> Bin Laden's voice was not heard on the tape.[27] [*Author's
> note*: Although this man's name is often, as here, translit-
> erated "al-Zawahiri," it evidently should be rendered
> "al-Zawahri."]

In other words, if bin Laden was indeed still alive and al-Qaeda
operatives wanted to assure the world of this fact, why did they not
put out a videotape on which bin Laden himself appeared and
spoke, referring to recent events?

PAKISTANI SOURCES

Still more support for bin Laden's death was provided on October
26, 2002, by a story on ArabicNews.com entitled "Pakistani Paper:
Bin Laden Is Dead." It said:

> The Paris-based "al-Watan al-Arabi" issued yesterday said
> that Pakistani sources confirmed the death of the leader
> of al-Qaida organization Osama Bin Laden as a result of
> the American air bombardment…, noting that the US
> hid the news of his death for fears of the escalation of
> voices which call for halting the international campaign
> against terrorism and the withdrawal of the American
> forces.
>
> The same sources, in exclusive statement to the maga-
> zine in its recent issue, attributed the reasons behind
> Washington's hiding news on the death of Osama Bin
> Laden to the desire of the hawks of the American admin-
> istration to use the issue of al-Qaida and international
> terrorism to invade Iraq, expecting that the death of Bin
> Laden will be only announced after completing the plan
> of attacking Iraq.[28]

Besides providing additional support for the belief that bin Laden
had been dead for many months, this story suggested a possible
explanation for why public expression of this belief by Bush admin-

istration figures, which had been somewhat common in 2002, would become less so in the following years.

A LULL, THEN FURTHER STATEMENTS FROM RUMSFELD

It appears, in fact, that during 2003 and most of 2004, few if any US officials or news agencies publicly stated that bin Laden might be dead. Apparently the first expression of doubt about bin Laden's continued existence by a US official after 2002 was on the third anniversary of 9/11. During a speech on September 11, 2004, Secretary of Defense Rumsfeld said that "[Osama bin Laden], if he's alive, is spending a whale of a lot of time trying to not get caught. And we've not seen him on a video since 2001."[29]

Rumsfeld addressed this issue again at the end of that month in an interview with Rita Crosby of Fox News. Referring to a suggestion that bin Laden might be dead made by a general at CENTCOM (the US Central Command) during a Fox News interview, Crosby asked: "What do you think?" Rumsfeld replied:

> Oh, goodness. You know, we have not seen him on video since 2001, in December, I think…. We don't know for sure if he's alive because we haven't seen him. Our assumption is he is alive. My further assumption—mine, as opposed to the [CIA's]—is that if he is alive, he would like to be on video and for some reason he's not.[30]

Although Rumsfeld expressed his belief that bin Laden was alive, his statement actually provided evidence to the contrary: Besides reiterating the fact that there had been no sighting of bin Laden since December 2001, Rumsfeld repeated the point made in Amir Taheri's 2002 *New York Times* article: If Osama bin Laden were alive, he would presumably want to appear on a video to demonstrate this fact.

DECLAN WALSH AND FORMER CIA ANALYST MICHAEL SCHEUER

Further inadvertent support for the demise of bin Laden was provided in a September 11, 2006, article by Declan Walsh in

London's *Guardian*. Although Walsh wrote on the assumption that bin Laden was still alive, he made four points that could be considered evidence for the opposing view.

First, Walsh quoted former CIA analyst Michael Scheuer, who had set up the CIA's bin Laden unit in 1996, as saying: "As far as I know there's been no serious credible information about his location since Tora Bora."

Second, besides citing *Le Figaro*'s report that bin Laden had gone to Dubai in 2001 for kidney treatment, Walsh mentioned that a Peshawar journalist, while interviewing bin Laden in 1998, had "noticed his copious consumption of water and green tea, which may indicate kidney disease."

Third, Walsh pointed out that "America's $25 million bounty [for bin Laden]—advertised on Pakistani television and hawked on cheap State Department matchboxes bearing his picture—remain[ed] untouched." Although he quoted a US official as explaining this strange fact by saying that Pakistanis "can't be bought," a more plausible explanation—in light of Walsh's observation that "51 percent of Pakistanis… support bin Laden," which implies that nearly half do not—might be that there was no Osama bin Laden to sell.

Finally, Walsh reported Scheuer's disclosure that the CIA had shut down its bin Laden unit—which would be a natural thing to do if the CIA knew, or at least was strongly convinced, that bin Laden was already dead.[31]

So, although Walsh, like virtually all other reporters who have dealt with this issue, wrote as if there were little doubt that bin Laden was still alive, he provided considerable evidence for the conclusion that he was dead.

THE RECENT COMMENTS BY BAER AND CODEVILLA REVISITED

For readers not previously familiar with the public discussion of this question, especially in 2001 and 2002, the comments quoted at the outset of this essay by former intelligence officers Robert Baer and Angelo Codevilla, which suggested that Osama bin Laden is probably dead, may have seemed baseless. As we have seen, however, their view is supported by considerable evidence.

In the early years after the 9/11 attacks, this view had been suggested by several people familiar with the facts. The idea that bin Laden *might* have died in 2001 was suggested by Keith Kenton (the first commander of the US-led coalition in Afghanistan), Secretary of Defense Donald Rumsfeld, and reportedly even President Bush. The idea that bin Laden had *probably* died was expressed by FBI counterterrorism chief Dale Watson, by President Musharraf of Pakistan and President Karzai of Afghanistan, by sources within Israeli intelligence, and (implicitly) by Dr. Sanjay Gupta. The idea that bin Laden had *definitely* died was expressed by Pakistani sources (who reported his funeral), Amir Taheri (in an essay considered worthy of publication by the *New York Times*), and by Oliver North.

Baer's report about his poll of CIA officers assigned to track bin Laden—that he did not find a single one who was certain that bin Laden was still alive—becomes less surprising after one reads that Oliver North had, back in 2002, reported that "all the other guys [he stayed] in touch with" shared his certainty that bin Laden was already dead.

Finally, although in recent years the press had, prior to the statements by Baer in late 2008 and Codevilla in early 2009, carried few if any stories suggesting that bin Laden might be dead—a fact that probably made Baer's statement on NPR surprising to many listeners—back in 2001 and 2002 such stories had been frequently carried by television networks and print publications, including CNN, CBS, Fox News, *Time*, the *New York Times*, and the *Telegraph*.

Why was there, between 2002 and Baer's 2008 statement, virtually no public discussion of the possibility that bin Laden had died in December 2001? One possible reason would be that, after 2002, good evidence that bin Laden was still alive showed up, laying to rest the speculation that he had died. Evidence of this nature, consisting mainly of audiotapes and videotapes purportedly from bin Laden, certainly did show up, as we will see below.

Baer's statement, however, did not reflect ignorance of the existence of such tapes. It instead reflected his conviction that these tapes were probably inauthentic. After saying "Of course he's dead," he added:

> Where are the DVDs?... All these things can be manipulated, as you know. Voices can be manipulated. We can take this recording and you can change everything so that it was completely the opposite of what I said. Your technicians could do this.[32]

Still more recently, referring to the tapes purportedly put out by bin Laden since 9/11, Baer said:

> Experts will tell you that off-the-shelf digital-editing software could manipulate old bin Laden voice recordings to make it sound as if he were discussing current events.[33]

Angelo Codevilla also expressed his conviction about bin Laden's demise while being fully aware of the tapes. He wrote:

> The audio and video tapes alleged to be Osama's never convinced impartial observers. The guy just does not look like Osama. Some videos show him with a Semitic aquiline nose, while others show him with a shorter, broader one. Nor does the tapes' Osama sound like Osama. ... Above all, ... the words on the Osama tapes differ substantively from what the real Osama used to say.[34]

I turn next to the question of whether Baer and Codevilla are right, or whether, to the contrary, some of the *proffered* evidence for bin Laden's continued existence was *good* evidence.

The question of whether any of the tapes attributed to Osama bin Laden provided good evidence that he was still alive is the same, of course, as the question of whether any of them could withstand critical examination based on the suspicion that they had been fabricated. Such a suspicion was voiced, as we saw, by sources within Israeli intelligence in 2002, who said that, because bin Laden had likely died in 2001, "the emergence of new messages by Bin Laden are probably fabrications."[35] There is, we will see, much additional evidence to support this suspicion.

2

Two Fake bin Laden Videos in 2001?

One reason to suspect the post-2001 "messages from bin Laden" to be fabrications would be the good evidence that some of the messages that appeared already in 2001 were inauthentic. And there are, in fact, good reasons to believe that two "bin Laden videos"—one that actually appeared and one that was merely reported—were fabricated in late 2001.

The "October Video" Reported in November 2001

On November 11, 2001, London's *Telegraph* published an article by David Bamber with the provocative title "Bin Laden: Yes, I Did It." According to Bamber, the *Telegraph* had on the previous day "obtained access" to the footage of "a previously undisclosed video" in which "Osama bin Laden has for the first time admitted that his al-Qa'eda group carried out the [9/11] attacks." Saying that this video had been "circulating for 14 days among [bin Laden's] supporters"—which would have meant since October 28, 2001—Bamber wrote:

> In the footage, shot in the Afghan mountains at the end of October, a smiling bin Laden goes on to say that the World Trade Centre's twin towers were a "legitimate target" and the pilots who hijacked the planes were "blessed by Allah."[1]

Publishing his piece on a Sunday, Bamber wrote: "The video will form the centrepiece of Britain and America's new evidence against bin Laden, to be released this Wednesday."[2]

However, when Wednesday—which was November 14, 2001—came, the video was *not* presented. This was because, Prime Minister

Tony Blair explained, the British government did not have a copy of it. Nor did Blair provide, or even claim to have, a complete transcript of the video. Rather, he merely read some statements that were said to have been made by bin Laden in the video, including a statement that he (bin Laden) had "instigated" the 9/11 attacks. Afterward, the British government published some "transcript excerpts of the video" on its website.[3] Why so little? According to a *Washington Post* story:

> The British government did not release the video or a full transcript, saying it does not have a copy of the video but has information about it from intelligence sources.[4]

This was a surprising development, especially in light of Bamber's story three days earlier, according to which the *Telegraph* had "obtained access" to the video. Were people to believe that, although "intelligence sources" and the *Telegraph* had obtained a copy of, or at least seen, the video, the British government was unable to obtain the same level of access—and could not even acquire a complete transcript?

It is hard to know what to make of this episode. Surely, if the *Telegraph* had obtained a video on which, for the first time, bin Laden clearly confessed to having instigated the 9/11 attacks, this newspaper would not—it *could* not—have refused to give a copy to the British government. It is also difficult to imagine under what circumstances British intelligence sources in the field would have obtained access to such a video and yet not sent a copy to government officials in London. And if the government had such a video, it surely would have made it, or at least portions of it, available to the public. It would have done this, that is, unless the video was a fake and the government decided, between November 11 and 14, that the fakery was so obvious that it should deny having a copy while merely releasing damning "excerpts."

This explanation is, of course, merely one possibility among many. But the strangeness of the episode at least raises a reasonable suspicion that a fake "bin Laden confession video" had been made.

The grounds for this suspicion are increased by circumstances surrounding Blair's announcement. The previous month, on October 4, Blair had provided something that the Bush administration had refused to supply after having promised to do so: a document containing evidence that Osama bin Laden was responsible for the 9/11 attacks.[5] Blair's document, listing "clear conclusions reached by the government," stated: "Osama Bin Laden and al-Qaeda, the terrorist network which he heads, planned and carried out the atrocities on 11 September 2001."[6] However, claiming that the government's best evidence for bin Laden's guilt was "too sensitive to release," this document began with a significant caveat—that it did "not purport to provide a prosecutable case against Osama Bin Laden in a court of law."[7]

The weakness of the evidence presented by the Blair government's document, which was implicitly acknowledged in this caveat, was explicitly pointed out the following day by the BBC. In a report entitled "The Investigation and the Evidence," the BBC said: "There is no direct evidence in the public domain linking Osama Bin Laden to the 11 September attacks. At best the evidence is circumstantial."[8]

Could the embarrassment caused to the Blair government by this development have led someone to try to bolster its case by fabricating a video that would seemingly provide the "powerful and incontrovertible" evidence that Blair had promised?[9] The fact that Blair's ongoing attempt to provide such evidence provided part of the context for his November 14 announcement of the new bin Laden video was acknowledged in the *Washington Post* article, which said:

> Expanding on a previous summary of evidence [for bin Laden's guilt] that he issued on Oct. 4, [Blair] declared that [in light of the new video] "there is no doubt whatever of the guilt of bin Laden and his associates."

Moreover, after pointing out that most Muslims in Britain did not believe that bin Laden was responsible for the 9/11 attacks and suspected instead that he had been "set up as a scapegoat by Washington and London," this article stated:

> In an attempt to counter such skepticism, Blair has func-
> tioned as the U.S.-led anti-terrorism coalition's chief
> prosecutor, often releasing more details than have U.S.
> officials.[10]

Could someone in US or British intelligence, with or without Blair's
knowledge, have fabricated a video to assist his efforts?

Suspicion about the authenticity of the reported video could be
further fostered by still another feature of the timing of Blair's
announcement. The concluding paragraph of Bamber's November
11 article said:

> Emergency powers to imprison suspected international
> terrorists indefinitely using special closed courts will be
> announced this week. The measure, which will require
> exemption from human rights legislation, will be used
> to round up about 20 suspects hiding in Britain beyond
> the reach of existing laws.[11]

Was it not suspiciously convenient that a video, in which bin Laden
for the first time confessed his responsibility for 9/11, showed up
just in time to support this new legislation?

In any case, while it is impossible to determine, on the basis of
the evidence that has been made public, what really lay behind this
strange episode, it seems likely that a fabrication of some sort
occurred, because if a genuine bin Laden confession video had been
obtained, the British government would almost certainly have made
it public. Perhaps a fake video was made and then never broadcast.
Or the fabrication could have been simply the claim that a bin
Laden confession video existed.

In either case, the incident suggests that the fabrication of
evidence to support the US and UK governments' claims about bin
Laden had occurred already in 2001.

THE VIDEO DATED NOVEMBER 9, 2001

On December 13, 2001, the Pentagon released a video that it said
had been found by US forces in a private home in Jalalabad,

Afghanistan, in late November, after anti-Taliban forces had taken over the city. A label on the tape reportedly indicated that it had been made on November 9, 2001. The tape purportedly shows Osama bin Laden, in a private home, talking about the 9/11 attacks with a visiting sheikh. During the course of the conversation, in which the bin Laden figure is seen and heard gloating about the success of the attacks, he states that he not only knew about them several days in advance but had also, in fact, planned them.[12]

Claims That the Video Proved bin Laden's Guilt: American and British officials declared that this tape removed any possible doubt about bin Laden's responsibility for 9/11. A *Washington Post* story reported that according to government officials, this videotape "offers the most conclusive evidence of a connection between bin Laden and the Sept. 11 attacks."[13] President Bush declared: "For those who see this tape, they'll realize that not only is [Osama bin Laden] guilty of incredible murder, he has no conscience and no soul."[14] Downing Street, according to the BBC, said that the video, by "showing Bin Laden boasting about the 11 September attacks, was conclusive proof of his involvement."[15] A BBC News article entitled "Tape 'Proves Bin Laden's Guilt'" quoted Jack Straw, the British foreign secretary, as saying: "By boasting about his involvement in the evil attacks, Bin Laden confirms his guilt."[16]

These claims were widely endorsed, at least by the American press corps. On PBS's *Newshour with Jim Lehrer*, for example, Ray Suarez introduced a discussion of the video with two guests by saying:

> Administration officials said they were convinced the tape was authentic.... Well, guests, we saw Osama bin Laden showing no remorse, no regret, exalting [*sic*] at the extent of his success.... [W]hat was your reaction?

One of these guests was Jessica Stern, the author of *The Ultimate Terrorists*, who said: "[I]t's completely horrifying to see him rejoicing about what happened." The other guest was Ahmed Rashid, the author of *Taliban*. Speaking as a Muslim, Rashid said: "I was quite horrified at the way that bin Laden and the associates used the name of Allah in association with such a horrendous act."

When Suarez asked "about those who… have expressed doubt about the connection between Osama bin Laden and the September 11 attacks," Rashid replied:

> This tape will certainly have an impact on a lot of skep-tics…. I think a major role now has to be played by leaders in the Arab world who have not openly, so far,… really condemned bin Laden…. [T]his tape… really offers irrefutable proof that he was behind it.

Stern said she "completely agree[d] with Ahmed."[17]

But the tape would constitute "irrefutable proof" only under two conditions. First, it would have to be authentic, meaning that the speaker really was Osama bin Laden. Second, bin Laden would have needed to be telling the truth, as opposed to making a "false confession," that is, taking credit for something he had not really planned, perhaps in order to attract recruits to al-Qaeda. The tape did, in fact, provide grounds for suspecting that this type of moti-vation might have lain behind its production: The bin Laden figure said that there had been a huge increase in the number of people converting to Islam since 9/11, to which the sheikh replied that, whereas the number of people following bin Laden prior to the "huge event" had been quite small, they were now coming by the hundreds.[18]

Although the second of these two problems should be kept in mind by journalists (who often make the mistake of assuming that a confession necessarily proves guilt), I will explore only the first problem: Might the video be a fake? Many people have thought so.

Claims That the Video Is a Fake: On December 14, 2001—the day after the Pentagon released this video—a BBC News report said: "Washington calls it the 'smoking gun' that puts Bin Laden's guilt beyond doubt, but many in the Arab world believe the home video of the al-Qaeda chief is a fake." This BBC report was, in fact, entitled: "Could the Bin Laden Video Be a Fake?"[19]

This question was also raised that same day in Canada by CBC News. In a story entitled "'Feeble' to Claim Bin Laden Tape Fake: Bush," CBC pointed out that some people had "suggested the Americans hired someone to pretend to be the exiled Saudi."[20]

This question was raised more insistently the following day in a *Guardian* story entitled "US Urged to Detail Origin of Tape." Reporting "growing doubt in the Muslim world about the authenticity of the film," writer Steven Morris said:

> The White House yesterday came under pressure to give more details of the video which purports to show Osama bin Laden admitting his part in the September 11 attacks.

The reason for the doubt was the fact that the White House had provided no details about how the Pentagon came to be in possession of the tape. As Morris put it:

> According to US officials the tape was found in a house in Jalalabad, eastern Afghanistan, and handed to the Pentagon by an unnamed person or group.... But for many the explanation is too convenient. Some opponents of the war theorise that the Bin Laden in the film was a look-alike.

Morris then quoted one such opponent, Riaz Durrani, a spokesman for a group that organized pro-Taliban rallies in Pakistan, who said: "This videotape is not authentic. The Americans made it up after failing to get any evidence against Osama." Morris also cited Bob Crabtree, the editor of *Computer Video* magazine, who explained that it was impossible to determine whether the video was authentic without more details of its source, adding: "The US seems simply to have asked the world to trust them that it is genuine."[21]

Both US and British officials did insist, of course, on the genuineness of the videotape. The British foreign secretary, Jack Straw, declared:

> There is no doubt it is the real thing. People are able to
> see Bin Laden there with those utterly chilling words of
> admission about his guilt for organising the atrocities of
> September 11.[22]

In spite of Straw's assurance, however, there *were* doubts, as we have
seen, because many people suspected that, rather than seeing bin
Laden himself on the tape, they were merely seeing someone who
looked like him.

President Bush gave a different response to skeptics, saying:

> It's preposterous for anybody to think that this tape is
> doctored. That's just a feeble excuse to provide weak
> support for an incredibly evil man.... Those who
> contend it's a farce or a fake are hoping for the best about
> an evil man.[23]

But Bush's *ad hominem* argument, like Straw's bare assertion, failed
to reply to the legitimate reasons people have expressed for doubting
the tape's authenticity. I turn now to such reasons.

Was Fabricating the Tape Technically Possible?: The first question, of
course, is whether the technical capacity to fabricate such a videotape existed in 2001. Experts say that it did. In his *Guardian* article,
Steven Morris wrote:

> Sean Broughton, director of the London-based produc-
> tion company Smoke and Mirrors and one of Britain's
> leading experts on visual effects, said it would be rela-
> tively easy for a skilled professional to fake a video of Bin
> Laden.

Morris also quoted John Henry Hingson, former president of the
National Association of Criminal Defense Lawyers, as saying: "In
this day and age of digital wizardry, many things can be done to
alter [a videotape's] veracity."[24]

The BBC News article dealing with the possibility of fabrication
cited John Gibbons, a linguist at the University of Sydney, as saying

that one test of authenticity would be whether the lips and the voice were synchronized.[25] The BBC pointed out that they were, but added that such synchronization is "not conclusive proof" of authenticity.

To explain one reason why not, Morris, paraphrasing Sean Broughton, described how a synchronized fake video could be produced:

> The first step would be to transfer images shot on video-tape on to film tape.… A "morphing package" would then be used to manipulate the image on a computer screen. Using such a package it is possible to alter the subject's mouth and expressions to fit in with whatever soundtrack is desired.[26]

Could a fake bin Laden video have been good enough for the fabrication to be undetectable? Dr. Peter French, a forensic expert who specializes in audio, speech, and language, was quoted by the BBC as saying: "[T]oday, using digital equipment, it's possible to edit or fabricate in ways that completely defy forensic detection."[27]

If it was technically possible for the bin Laden video to have been fabricated, the next question is whether there are any reasons to believe that it actually was. I will discuss several.

Would bin Laden Have Allowed His Confession to Be Taped? According to the US government's statement on the document containing its translation of the video, the comments made by Osama bin Laden and others "were video taped with the knowledge of Bin Laden and all present."[28] But why would bin Laden have allowed this? As the Taliban regime's former defense minister said, "it was unlikely that Bin Laden would have been naive enough to say such things on a recording."[29]

With regard to this question, the *Washington Post* wrote: "U.S. intelligence officials are not certain as to why the tape was shot, but in other cases such tapes have been used by al Qaeda for recruitment purposes, a senior official said."[30] As we saw earlier, there is support for this suggestion on the tape, as the bin Laden figure and his conversation partner discussed the fact that interest in Islam in general and bin Laden's movement in particular had increased greatly since the 9/11 attacks.

This explanation for the tape, however, faces a difficult problem. If bin Laden had planned the 9/11 attacks and then allowed himself to be taped boasting about them, so that the tape could be used for recruitment purposes, we would assume that he would not have consistently denied, until a few days before this tape was reportedly made, being responsible for the attacks. And yet he did.

On September 12, the day immediately after the attacks, one of his aides told Al-Jazeera that, although bin Laden "thanked Almighty Allah and bowed before him when he heard this news," he had "had no information or knowledge about the attack."[31]

Four days later, on September 16, bin Laden told Al-Jazeera: "I stress that I have not carried out this act, which appears to have been carried out by individuals with their own motivation."[32]

The following day, September 17, bin Laden sent the Afghan Islamic Press a statement saying: "I am residing in Afghanistan. I have taken an oath of allegiance to [Mullah Omar] which does not allow me to do such things from Afghanistan. We have been blamed in the past, but we were not involved."[33]

On September 28, in response to the question of whether he had been involved in 9/11, he replied:

> I have already said that I am not involved in the 11 September attacks in the United States. As a Muslim, I try my best to avoid telling a lie. I had no knowledge of these attacks, nor do I consider the killing of innocent women, children and other humans as an appreciable act. Islam strictly forbids causing harm to innocent women, children and other people. Such a practice is forbidden even in the course of a battle.... [W]e are against the American system, not against its people, whereas in these attacks, the common American people have been killed.[34]

In a videotape of October 7, 2001, just after the first US strikes on Afghanistan, bin Laden praised the "vanguards of Islam… [who] destroyed America," but he did not himself claim responsibility for the attacks.[35]

In a videotape broadcast November 3, bin Laden's only reference to 9/11 was this statement: "[N]o evidence links what happened in the United States to the people of Afghanistan. The people of Afghanistan have nothing to do with this matter."[36]

Would it not be strange if bin Laden, after this series of statements, suddenly allowed himself on November 9 to be videotaped gloating about his successful planning of the 9/11 attacks, so that this video could be used to recruit people to al-Qaeda? If bin Laden believed that openly admitting his responsibility for 9/11 would be a good recruiting tool, why would he have waited two months to do so?

Also, if bin Laden had orchestrated the attacks and had been planning to confess this fact, would he have made the statement of September 28—in which he denied responsibility for the attacks while adding that, as a Muslim, he tried his best not to lie— knowing that shortly thereafter everyone would know that he had been lying in the very act of making that statement? Would he have stressed that Islam forbids killing innocent human beings—which, he clearly indicated, the people in the Twin Towers were?

I turn now to the fact that, to accept the authenticity of the video of November 9, 2001, one must accept not only a sudden change in bin Laden's testimony about 9/11 but also a striking change in his appearance.

The Appearance of "bin Laden" in the November 9 Video: There are three undoubtedly authentic videos of bin Laden with which to compare the one reportedly made on November 9. Two of them were filmed shortly before that date, these being the aforementioned videos of October 7 and November 3. In both of these videos, there is a considerable amount of white in bin Laden's beard. But in the one from October 7, he appears to be fairly healthy,[37] while in the one from November 3, his health appears to have deteriorated somewhat.[38]

We also have the video that was filmed *after* November 9. This is the previously discussed video that was released December 27, although it was probably filmed somewhat earlier. We know, in any case, that it was filmed later than the November 9 video, because in it bin Laden referred to an event that had occurred on November 16.

In this post–November 16 video, bin Laden's health appeared to have deteriorated still further: The *Telegraph*, as we saw, described him as having a "gaunt, frail appearance," adding that his "beard was much whiter than on November 3." Dr. Sanjay Gupta spoke of "his paleness of skin" and "very gaunt sort of features," which suggested "chronic illness."

Given these three videos, in which bin Laden's health appeared to keep deteriorating, we would expect the bin Laden of the video dated November 9 to have appeared about the same, or even somewhat worse, than bin Laden appeared in the November 3 video.

That, however, is not what we find. The bin Laden of this "confession video" seems much darker than the pale bin Laden of the previous videos and the post–November 16 video.[39] He also seems to be heavier and to have fuller cheeks than not only the "gaunt, frail" bin Laden of the post–November 16 video but also the bin Laden of the November 3 video. Are we to believe that bin Laden, who had apparently deteriorated somewhat between the October 7 and November 3 videos, suddenly by November 9 became heavier and healthier than he had been on October 7, only to deteriorate even more by the time the post–November 16 video was made?

And there are three more problems. First, the bin Laden of this "confession video," besides being heavier and darker than the bin Laden of the videos that came before and after it, also seemed to have a differently shaped nose.[40] A second problem is that he also appeared to have shorter, heavier hands than the real bin Laden.[41] A third problem is that, although the real bin Laden was left-handed, the "bin Laden" in the November 9 video can be briefly seen writing with his right hand. It might be thought that this was because his left arm, which was evidently immobile by the time the post–November 16 video was made, had already become immobile by the time the November 9 video was made. But the man in this video was easily able to lift his left arm above his head.[42]

Statements the Real bin Laden Would Not Have Made: At least equally serious is the fact that, while confessing to having planned the 9/11 attacks, the bin Laden of this "confession video" made some statements that the real bin Laden, if he had planned the attacks, would not have made.

One problem was contained in a statement in which the speaker, while referring to the hijackers, said:

> The brothers, who conducted the operation, all they knew was that they have a martyrdom operation… but they didn't know anything about the operation, not even one letter. But they were trained and we did not reveal the operation to them until they are there and just before they boarded the planes.[43]

If he meant that they did not know that they were to board those planes until the last minute, that would contradict the evidence that the nineteen men purchased their plane tickets two weeks in advance.[44]

Perhaps, however, he only meant that, although the men knew in advance that they were to board these planes, they did not know that they were to hijack and then crash them into the Twin Towers, the Pentagon, and one other target. But even this claim would be absurd. If the hijacker pilots did not learn their targets until "just before they boarded the planes," how could they have found their way to those targets with no assistance from air traffic control? Even if they used handheld GPS (global positioning system) units, as has been suggested, they would have needed to know the coordinates of their targets. In fact, a "bin Laden video" that appeared on September 9, 2002, which is discussed below, showed the alleged hijackers, as the BBC reported, "reading flight manuals and studying maps, one of which is of the Washington DC area."[45]

Accordingly, if bin Laden had really planned the operation, he would not have said that the hijackers did not know "one letter" about the operation until "just before they boarded the planes."

The confession video's bin Laden also said: "Those who were trained to fly didn't know the others. One group of people did not know the other group." The FBI reported, however, that the men said to have been the pilots and those called "muscle hijackers" mingled with each other. According to FBI testimony to the House and Senate permanent select committees on intelligence, some of the so-called muscle hijackers settled in Fort Lauderdale, along with pilots Mohamed Atta, Marwan al-Shehhi, and Ziad Jarrah, and the other muscle hijackers settled in Paterson, New Jersey, along with pilot Hani Hanjour.[46]

The bin Laden of this video made still another statement that the real bin Laden surely would not have made, saying:

> [W]e calculated in advance the number of casualties from the enemy who would be killed based on the position of the tower.... [D]ue to my experience in this field, I was thinking that the fire from the gas in the plane would melt the iron structure of the building and collapse the area where the plane hit and all the floors above it only. This is all that we had hoped for.[47]

There are two reasons why the real bin Laden, assuming he planned the attacks, would not have made this statement.

In the first place, given his experience as a contractor, he would have known that the buildings were framed with steel, not with iron. In the second place, and more seriously, he would have known that none of the buildings' steel (or iron) would have been melted by the "fire from the gas in the plane." He would have known that a building fire fed by jet fuel is a hydrocarbon fire, and that as such it could not, even under the most ideal conditions, have gotten above 1,800 degrees Fahrenheit (1,000 degrees Celsius). He would also have known that iron and steel do not begin to melt until they are heated to about 2,800 degrees Fahrenheit (1,540 degrees

Celsius). The real bin Laden, therefore, would not have expected any iron or steel to melt.

To summarize: We have seen that, besides the fact that this videotape *could have*, from a technical point of view, been fabricated, there are good reasons to believe that it *actually was* fabricated: (1) Bin Laden probably would not have allowed himself to be taped confessing his responsibility for the attacks, especially after having repeatedly denied such responsibility. (2) If bin Laden had indeed been responsible for the attacks and had planned to claim responsibility for them for recruitment purposes, he would not have made some of the statements he made in his denials, especially the September 28 statement that Islam forbids killing innocents. (3) The bin Laden figure in this video, besides appearing to be right-handed, also seemed, in comparison with the bin Laden of the videos made before and after November 9, to have been too dark, too heavy, and too healthy. (4) This man also said several things that the real bin Laden would surely not have said. Accordingly, there are at least four features of the videotape itself that suggest it is probably a fake.

There are also other reasons to reach this conclusion.

Possible Motives for Fabricating the Video: We saw above that, at the time of the bin Laden video of October 2001, which was reported but never produced by the *Telegraph* and the Blair government, there were circumstances for suspecting this video—or the very claim about its existence—to have been fabricated: Tony Blair had recently tried but failed to present convincing evidence of bin Laden's responsibility for 9/11, and he was also ready to announce emergency measures, which would override human rights legislation, to imprison suspected terrorists.

Similar circumstances surrounded the announcement in December 2001 of the November 9 video, as news stories at the time pointed out. In a Pulitzer prize–winning *Washington Post* story, Walter Pincus and Karen DeYoung, just before reporting that government officials called the videotape "the most conclusive evidence of a connection between bin Laden and the Sept. 11 attacks," said:

> The administration has blamed bin Laden for the Sept.
> 11 attacks but has not released evidence showing that he
> directly planned or ordered them. Although officials
> have said they have intercepted communications
> allegedly tying bin Laden or his associates to the hijack-
> ers, they have not released any such material.[48]

After saying that the decision about whether to release the information on the tape was reportedly being left up to presidential
counselor Karen Hughes (the *Post* story was published on December
9, four days before the videotape was actually released), Pincus and
DeYoung also provided this context:

> Shortly after the September terrorist attacks, President
> Bush gave Hughes the task of managing the White
> House information flow on the Afghan war. Hughes
> heads a special White House-based public relations
> operation that the United States and Britain began
> early last month to win international public support,
> particularly in the Islamic world, for the anti-terrorist
> campaign.
>
> The public relations group has been concerned with
> the lack of U.S. credibility in the Muslim world, and
> recent discussions about release of the tape have focused
> on how to get Arab audiences to believe its contents.[49]

People involved with this "public relations operation" certainly
would have had a powerful motive to produce a videotape that
would be widely regarded as providing "conclusive proof" of bin
Laden's responsibility for 9/11.

That such a motive might have existed was also indicated in the
BBC report entitled "Tape 'Proves Bin Laden's Guilt,'" which was
aired the day after the videotape's release. It said:

> The tape is being seen by America's allies as vindicating
> the US-led military campaign in Afghanistan…. The

White House hopes the video will bolster international support for the war on terrorism.[50]

Accordingly, whereas there seems to be no good answer to the question as to why bin Laden and his associates would have made this videotape, there would be no mystery about why forces within the Bush administration would have been motivated to do.

What Does the FBI Think of This Videotape? President Bush, as we saw, responded to skepticism about the authenticity of the tape by saying, "It is preposterous for anybody to think that this tape is doctored," and by portraying "[t]hose who contend it's a farce or a fake" as naïve because they were "hoping for the best about an evil man." Those who have questioned the tape's authenticity, however, would seem to include the Department of Justice and the FBI.

The FBI's website on "Usama bin Laden" as a "Most Wanted Terrorist" does not list 9/11 as one of the terrorist acts for which he is wanted.[51] In 2006, Rex Tomb, the FBI's chief of investigative publicity, was asked why not. He replied: "The reason why 9/11 is not mentioned on Usama Bin Laden's Most Wanted page is because the FBI has no hard evidence connecting Bin Laden to 9/11."[52] Explaining that the FBI cannot list people as "wanted" until they have been formally indicted by the Department of Justice, Tomb further said:

> The FBI gathers evidence. Once evidence is gathered, it is turned over to the Department of Justice. The Department of Justice then decides whether it has enough evidence to present to a federal grand jury. In the case of the 1998 United States Embassies being bombed, Bin Laden has been formally indicted and charged by a grand jury. He has not been formally indicted and charged in connection with 9/11 because the FBI has no hard evidence connecting Bin Laden to 9/11.[53]

If the FBI and the DOJ considered the "bin Laden confession video" of November 9 authentic, they would probably consider it "hard evidence" of bin Laden's connection to the 9/11 attacks. We can only assume, therefore, that the FBI and the DOJ do *not* consider it authentic. We can add this consideration to the previous grounds for concluding that it is a fake.

The Opinion of Professor Bruce Lawrence: In February 2007, Bruce Lawrence, a Duke University history professor who is widely considered the country's leading academic bin Laden expert,[54] was asked what he thought about this so-called confession video. Mincing no words, he said, bluntly, "It's bogus." Adding that he had some friends in the US Department of Homeland Security assigned to work "on the 24/7 bin Laden clock," he said that "they also know it's bogus." When asked why they do not make an open disavowal, he replied: "In some quarters, it really is convenient to say this guy did it all."[55]

A defender of the authenticity of this "bin Laden video" has claimed that Lawrence was talking about a later one. Lawrence, however, made clear that it was this one to which he was referring, calling it the "bogus smoking-gun tape that came out in November 2001."[56]

We have, in sum, an abundance of reasons for considering the so-called November 9 video a fake.

3

PURPORTED BIN LADEN MESSAGES AFTER 2001

The main question of this book is whether there is any good reason to believe that Osama bin Laden is still alive and, in particular, whether any of the purported bin Laden messages that have appeared since 2001 proved him to be still alive. What we have seen thus far is that fake bin Laden videos were evidently being issued already in November and early December of 2001, when bin Laden was clearly still alive. This fact gives us reason to be sufficiently suspicious of all post-2001 messages—both messages purportedly from bin Laden himself and messages from others reporting him to be still alive—to look at them with a critical eye. I turn now to a number of these later messages, including all those generally considered the most important.

THE E-MAIL MESSAGE OF MARCH 2002

On March 28, 2002, BBC News put out a story entitled "Paper 'Receives Bin Laden E-mail,'" which began:

> An Arabic newspaper [*Al-Quds al-Arabi*] based in London says it has received an e-mail purporting to have come from Osama Bin Laden.
>
> It is unclear whether the e-mail, which paid tribute to Palestinian suicide attacks against Israel as well as the 11 September attacks on the United States, was genuine.
>
> If so, it would be the first proof that Bin Laden had survived US bombing raids against the Taleban and al-Qaeda networks in Afghanistan.

In sections headed "Possible Forgery" and "Tracing E-Mail," the BBC story said:

> There has been no proven message from Bin Laden since
> the height of the Afghan war, and in March, Washington
> said it did not know whether he was dead or alive. The
> newspaper's editor, Abdel Bari Atwan, said he believed
> the message was from Bin Laden…. *Al-Quds Al-Arabi*
> did not give the sender's e-mail address or what steps it
> took to authenticate the message.[1]

So, although the recipient of the e-mail message evidently considered it authentic, he provided no basis for others to confirm his opinion.

THE JUNE 2002 MESSAGE FROM AL-QAEDA

On June 23, 2002, an Associated Press writer published a story entitled "Bin Laden Alive, Promises New Attacks and TV Address, Says Al-Qaida Spokesman." It began:

> Osama bin Laden is alive and well and will soon make an
> appearance, a man introduced as the spokesman for his
> al-Qaida terror network says in an interview appearing as
> an audio file on two Islamic Websites.

Saying that the interview had apparently been recorded recently and that the man seemed really to be who he purported to be—Salaiman Abu Ghaith, "the Kuwaiti-born spokesman for bin Laden"—the Associated Press writer quoted him as saying:

> I want to assure Muslims that Sheik Osama bin
> Laden… is in good and prosperous health and all what
> is being rumored about his illness and injury in Tora
> Bora has no truth.[2]

Besides supporting the US position on this point, the man claiming to be Abu Ghaith also backed up then-recent statements from US officials warning of new al-Qaeda attacks, stating: "I say 'Yes' to what American officials are saying—that we are going to carry out attacks on America. Yes, we will carry out attacks."

This man also supported the Bush administration's position on

9/11, affirming that al-Qaeda had been responsible not only—as the FBI's website on bin Laden as a "Most Wanted Terrorist" says—for the 1998 bombings of the US embassies in Kenya and Tanzania and the 2000 attack on the USS *Cole*, but also—as the FBI's website does *not* say—the attacks of September 11, 2001.

However, the Associated Press writer added: "The authenticity of the interview could not be verified."

One problem with the speaker's claims was that, if bin Laden had indeed not been killed in Tora Bora but was instead "alive and well," why did the speaker not bring a recording in which bin Laden, by referring to some recent event, proved his continued existence?

The self-proclaimed spokesman for bin Laden did, to be sure, promise such proof in the near future, saying that bin Laden would soon make a televised appearance. But no such appearance occurred.

THE SEPTEMBER 2002 VIDEOTAPE WITH "BIN LADEN'S VOICE"

On September 9 and 10, 2002, just before the first anniversary of the 9/11 attacks, Al-Jazeera television played excerpts from a videotape on which the voice of a man, claiming to be Osama bin Laden and speaking over the video footage, praised the nineteen alleged hijackers. Was it really the voice of bin Laden?

According to CNN, it almost certainly was. Although the opening paragraph of its report on the tape said that it was "purportedly of Osama bin Laden," the remainder of its story showed no such caution, simply attributing all of the statements on the tape to bin Laden. CNN stated, for example: "'There aren't enough words to describe how great these men were and how great their deeds were,' bin Laden said in an audiotape message." Given this certainty that the voice really was that of bin Laden, CNN concluded that the tape "left no doubt that al Qaeda was behind the terror attacks."

CNN did admit that "U.S. authorities have said they are unsure whether bin Laden is dead or alive." But immediately following this statement, the CNN story added: "Sources have told CNN that bin Laden... is alive in the frontier region of Pakistan near the Afghan border."[3]

A *Guardian* story by Brian Whitaker showed much greater journalistic caution. Besides speaking of Mohamed Atta as the "alleged hijacker," Whitaker referred to "the voice attributed to Bin Laden," and then added: "There was nothing to indicate that the sound-only recording attributed to Bin Laden had been made since the war in Afghanistan."[4]

The BBC was also properly circumspect. It agreed with other news media that "the voice [on the audiotape] sounds very similar to previous recordings of the al-Qaeda leader." But it then added that the tape "did not feature any video of Bin Laden apart from archive footage" and that "[t]he fate of Bin Laden... is still unknown."[5]

Between them, therefore, the BBC and the *Guardian* made clear that this tape offered no good evidence that bin Laden was still alive.

THE SATELLITE DETECTION REPORT OF OCTOBER 2002

On October 6, 2002, the *Guardian* published a story, which had been filed from Jalalabad by Jason Burke, entitled "Bin Laden Still Alive, Reveals Spy Satellite." Burke's story began:

> Osama bin Laden is alive and regularly meeting Mullah Omar, the fugitive leader of the Taliban, according to a telephone call intercepted by American spy satellites.
>
> In the conversation, recorded less than a month ago, Omar and a senior aide were discussing the American-led hunt to track them down. The two men, using a mobile Thuraya satellite phone, spoke about tactics for several minutes. Omar then turned to a third person who was within a few yards of him, voice analysis has revealed. After exchanging a few words, Omar said that "the sheikh sends his salaams [greetings]." Senior Taliban figures habitually refer to bin Laden as "the sheikh."
>
> Voice analysis appears to corroborate the identification of bin Laden. "It shows he was alive recently at least," said a senior Afghan intelligence officer. "Some people might like to think he is dead, but that's just wishful thinking."[6]

Although this story might appear to have provided solid grounds to believe that bin Laden was still alive in September 2002, it contained no confirmable evidence. What was the basis for Burke's assertion that the conversation with Omar was intercepted by a US satellite? Did he hear the conversation or simply take the word of a US intelligence officer?

Indeed, Burke himself supplied a reason to suspect that bin Laden could not really have been spotted, saying:

> The revelation comes amid growing speculation that bin Laden is dead. He has looked gaunt and unwell in videos released by al-Qaeda, and appeared unable to use his left arm. There has been no public statement from bin Laden since early this year. Some analysts say this lack of communication indicates that he might be dead.

In referring to "growing speculation that bin Laden is dead," Burke, writing early in October 2002, might have been alluding to the aforementioned spate of reports—from major media such as CBS, CNN, *Time* magazine, and the *New York Times* and about people such as Dale Watson and Oliver North—suggesting that bin Laden was no longer alive. Could someone in the US intelligence services have decided it was time for a revelation from on high to dampen down such reports?

Moreover, even if the reported conversation really was intercepted, readers were not told who it was that carried out the voice analysis to confirm that the "sheikh" really was bin Laden. Burke simply referred to an unnamed "senior Afghan intelligence officer." Moreover, even if bin Laden's voice really was heard, how would readers know that this was not simply a recording made the previous December or earlier? Burke, in fact, pointed to the possibility of deception on Omar's part, saying: "[Some] analysts feel Omar could have been bluffing, knowing he was being listened to by the Americans."[7]

Accordingly, the "revelation" that Burke reported from Afghanistan did not really provide any good evidence that bin Laden was still alive.

It is interesting to note that October 7, 2002—the next day after Burke's story was published—was when Hamid Karzai, Afghanistan's president, told CNN that he believed bin Laden to be dead.[8]

In any case, another bin Laden audiotape would appear about six weeks later and be pronounced authentic by the most famous US intelligence agency, the CIA.

THE BIN LADEN AUDIOTAPE OF NOVEMBER 2002

On November 12, 2002, Al-Jazeera broadcast an audiotape on which a voice, purportedly that of Osama bin Laden, mentioned some recent attacks on Western targets. At first blush, it thereby "appeared to provide," as a British journalist cautiously put it, "the first concrete evidence that Bin Laden is still alive."[9] *New York Times* journalist James Risen, less cautiously stating that it actually provided such evidence, wrote on November 19:

> United States intelligence officials have concluded that a recently recorded audiotape that was broadcast on an Arab television network last week is genuine and contains the voice of Osama bin Laden, apparently ending months of debate in the government over whether the elusive terrorist leader is still alive.
>
> An American intelligence official said today that an "extensive analysis" of the audiotape conducted over several days had convinced intelligence experts that the tape "almost certainly" contained the voice of Mr. Bin Laden.[10]

This verdict that the tape was "almost certainly" authentic reflected the fact that intelligence officials said that a comparison of the voice on the videotape with past samples of bin Laden's voice did not produce "a 100 percent match," but "it came close."

Risen further bolstered his claim that the voice was almost certainly that of bin Laden by quoting more people who supported this conclusion. One of these was White House spokesman Scott McClellan, who said: "The intelligence experts do believe that the tape is genuine." Risen also quoted an unnamed intelligence official as saying: "At this point, there is no evidence to indicate and no reason to believe that the tape was manufactured or altered."

Risen then, on the basis of assurance by US intelligence experts that the voice was "almost certainly" that of bin Laden, offered his own assessment:

> The more definitive statement about the tape clearly shows that the United States intelligence agencies, once divided over whether the Saudi exile had survived last year's war in Afghanistan, has now reached a consensus that he is still at large.

Next, quoting Senate Intelligence Committee vice chairman Richard Shelby's statement that the message bin Laden was "trying to get out… to the world is, 'I'm alive,'" Risen commented:

> The tape offers the first hard evidence of that since last December, when Mr. bin Laden was overheard in intercepted radio transmissions giving orders to Qaeda fighters in the Tora Bora region of Afghanistan.

Finally, pointing out that some counterterrorism experts and even President Bush had concluded from bin Laden's long silence that he might be dead, Risen spoke of the "Saudi exile's re-emergence."[11]

Two writers for *Time* magazine evidently were equally persuaded by US intelligence professionals, saying that the tape provided "almost certain confirmation that bin Laden is alive."[12]

Given only these articles, based solely on sources within the US intelligence community, one might have assumed that the audiotape of November 12, 2002, had provided virtually conclusive proof that bin Laden was still alive.

Before that month ended, however, London's *Guardian* published an article with a title suggesting a radically different conclusion: "Swiss Scientists 95% Sure That Bin Laden Recording Was a Fake." The Swiss scientists, explained journalist Brian Whitaker, were "researchers at the Dalle Molle Institute for Perceptual Artificial Intelligence, in Lausanne," headed by voice recognition expert Hervé Bourlard, who had "worked extensively with the International Computer Science Institute at Berkeley, California."[13] The verdict of Bourlard's institute was also reported by an Associated Press story entitled "Bin Laden Tape a Fake, Swiss Lab Says," which pointed out that Bourlard had presented this conclusion in a report on French television.[14]

It is possible, however, that the *Guardian* article, in speaking of "95 percent" certainty, may have overstated Bourlard's claim, because his institute's written report said that the study did not allow one "to draw any definite (statistically significant) conclusions."[15] In an interview, moreover, Bourlard said: "The best we can say is it's full of doubt." He did say, nevertheless, that if he had to come down on one side or the other, he would say that the voice on the tape was *not* that of bin Laden.[16]

In sum, whereas US intelligence officials declared the voice on the recording was "almost certainly" that of bin Laden, the Swiss voice experts, who surely had a more disinterested perspective, concluded that it was probably not.

THE AUDIOTAPE OF FEBRUARY 2003

On February 11, 2003, when the United States was preparing for its attack on Iraq (which occurred on March 20, 2003), another audiotape purportedly from bin Laden was broadcast by Al-Jazeera. In this one, Muslims were encouraged "to fight any US-led attack on Iraq."[17]

This audiotape became well known because Secretary of State Colin Powell, while speaking to a Senate panel that day, referred to it even before Al-Jazeera had announced that it had received it.[18] Saying that he had seen a transcript, Powell claimed (falsely) that bin Laden had said in this message that he was "in partnership with Iraq."[19] Powell was thereby supporting the Bush administration's contention that Saddam Hussein and bin Laden had a working relationship.

CNN pointed out that the tape did not support Powell's claim, saying: "While the message called for Iraqis to fight, it did not express support for Saddam. Instead, it referred to Saddam's Baath party as 'infidels.'" The White House, nevertheless, portrayed the tape as proof of "a burgeoning alliance of terror."[20]

With regard to the tape's authenticity (which the claims by Powell and the White House presupposed), CNN merely said: "U.S. officials said the tape does seem to be from bin Laden, and that a technical analysis will be done."[21] A few days later, an unnamed US official told reporters that a technical analysis carried out by intelligence experts "tells us it is almost certainly bin Laden."[22]

This tape does not provide any internal reasons to consider it inauthentic. The speaker said the kinds of things one would have expected bin Laden to say at that time. He also quoted the Qur'an several times and referred to both God and the Prophet Muhammad.[23]

However, even if the voice on this videotape, besides saying the right things, was also shown by technical means to be a perfect match for bin Laden's voice (as known through undoubtedly authentic recordings), this would not prove that bin Laden was still alive when the tape was made. As Robert Baer, who worked as a CIA operative for many years, pointed out in a statement quoted above, "voices can be manipulated."

The technology for such manipulation is called "voice morphing." The idea of morphing was mentioned earlier, in the discussion of whether the videotape of November 9, 2001, could have been fabricated. There the discussion was about video morphing, which, along with photo morphing, is the best-known form of digital morphing because of films such as *Forrest Gump*, released in 1994, in which the title character, played by Tom Hanks, is seen shaking hands with President Kennedy. Thanks to the awareness of photo and video morphing, many people now know that *seeing* isn't necessarily *believing*. But by 2000, voice morphing had also been perfected sufficiently to make the voices of people say things that they had never said.

In a 1999 *Washington Post* article entitled "When Seeing and Hearing Isn't Believing," William Arkin illustrated this point by reporting a demonstration using the voice of General Carl Steiner, former commander of the US Special Operations Command.

Steiner's voice was heard to say: "Gentlemen! We have called you together to inform you that we are going to overthrow the United States government." Arkin also reported a similar demonstration using the voice of Colin Powell.[24]

Arkin then wrote: "Digital morphing—voice, video, and photo—has come of age, available for use in psychological operations," or "PSYOPS, as the military calls it." Whereas digital morphing is used in Hollywood for special effects,

> For covert operators in the U.S. military and intelligence agencies, it is a weapon of the future.... To a growing group of information war technologists, it is the nexus of fantasy and reality. Being able to manufacture convincing audio or video, they say, might be the difference in a successful military operation or coup.[25]

Arkin also brought out the implications of voice morphing in particular for our present subject. Saying that "[v]ideo and photo manipulation has already raised profound questions of authenticity for the journalistic world," he pointed out that the addition of voice morphing has intensified to the burden of determining whether an apparent message is authentic. Just as the possibility of photo and video manipulation means that "seeing isn't necessarily believing," Arkin quoted an expert in information warfare as saying that the development of voice morphing implies a new lesson: "hearing isn't either."

Judging by the journalistic world's response to the various "messages from bin Laden," however, that lesson, stated in 1999, appears not yet to have been learned.

The implication of this lesson for the case at hand is that, even if the voice on the February 2003 audiotape had been shown by independent, disinterested experts to be a perfect match for bin Laden's voice, this by itself would not prove that bin Laden was still alive at that time.

Moreover, reason for skepticism about the tape's authenticity arises from its timing—appearing as it did just as the administration, through Colin Powell, was making its case for an attack on Iraq.

THE "OCTOBER SURPRISE" BIN LADEN VIDEO OF 2004

As we saw earlier, Secretary of Defense Rumsfeld remarked twice in 2004—first on September 11 and again on September 29—that bin Laden had not been seen on videotape since 2001, so one could not say for sure, Rumsfeld pointed out, whether he was still alive. A month later, a videotape appeared in which a bin Laden figure directly addressed the people of the United States. It was broadcast by Al-Jazeera on October 29, 2004, just four days before the US presidential election (which occurred on November 2). An Associated Press story said that this videotape "offered evidence that bin Laden was still alive."

The more explicit purpose of this video was indicated by the title of the AP article: "Bin Laden, in Statement to U.S. People, Says He Ordered Sept. 11 Attacks." Strangely, this article said that it was on this video that bin Laden admitted "for the first time" that he had ordered the attacks. It said this in spite of mentioning that the bin Laden of the November 9, 2001, video had said that the destruction of the Twin Towers had "exceeded even his 'optimistic' calculations."[26]

In any case, although the AP story said that the "FBI and Justice Department had no immediate assessment of the tape" and a largely identical CBS story said that "[t]here was no immediate way to authenticate [this 2004] tape,"[27] both news organizations treated it as unquestionably authentic. Neither one even raised the question as to whether the person on the tape was really Osama bin Laden.

There were, however, good reasons for skepticism. I will point out several.

An Implausible Claim: One reason for skepticism about the authenticity of this tape was the bin Laden figure's claim that he first thought of attacking the Twin Towers back in 1982, "when the U.S. permitted the Israelis to invade Lebanon with the aid of the American sixth fleet." The speaker continued:

> I still remember those moving scenes—blood, torn
> limbs, and dead women and children; ruined homes
> everywhere, and high-rises being demolished on top of
> their residents…. As I was looking at those destroyed
> towers in Lebanon, I was struck by the idea of punishing
> the oppressor in the same manner and destroying towers
> in the U.S., to give it a taste of what we have tasted and
> to deter it from killing our children and women.[28]

Is this really believable—that Osama bin Laden had been planning to
attack the Twin Towers since 1982? If so, he should be known as not
only the world's greatest terrorist but also its greatest procrastinator.

Could bin Laden Have Become Younger? An even more serious
problem is that, like the bin Laden of the confession video of
November 9, 2001, the bin Laden of this 2004 confession video
appeared to have become younger and healthier. This problem was
pointed out by Bahukutumbi Raman, a former government official
in India, who asked:

> Is it [the video] genuine? How come OBL seems to be
> growing younger and healthier, when, like all human
> beings, he should be growing older and weaker, particu-
> larly when he is being relentlessly hunted, as we are told
> day in and day out by Bush?[29]

A Rationalistic, Nonreligious Lecture: Raman also pointed out that
the bin Laden of this new video was also strikingly different in other
respects:

> The latest tape shows OBL not as a dreaded jihadi terror-
> ist hurling blood-curdling threats at the American
> people, against the background of rifles and the wildness
> of the Afghan terrain, but as a mujahideen statesman
> addressing well-reasoned arguments to the American
> people from behind a lectern in a TV studio-like
> ambiance,… appear[ing] like a man in the pink of his

health, in total control of his faculties and of the world around him, with no care in the world.[30]

Part and parcel of this different approach was the paucity of religious language in this 2004 message, compared with bin Laden messages that are undoubtedly authentic. For example, bin Laden's video of October 7, 2001, had begun with these phrases:

> Praise be to God and we beseech Him for help and forgiveness. We seek refuge with the Lord of our bad and evildoing. He whom God guides is rightly guided but he whom God leaves to stray, for him wilt thou find no protector to lead him to the right way. I witness that there is no God but God and Mohammed is His slave and Prophet.[31]

In this speech as a whole, which had only 725 words, bin Laden referred to God (Allah) twenty times and to Mohammed three times. Likewise, his message of November 3, 2001, which contained 2,333 words, began in the same way and referred to God 35 times and to Mohammed eight times.[32] By contrast, the 2004 message, which contained 2,240 words, mentioned God only twelve times, and the only "Muhammad" mentioned was Atta, the alleged ringleader of the 9/11 hijackers.

Moreover, not only the language of this 2004 message but also statements about causation were much less religious than the statements in the undoubtedly authentic messages. For example, bin Laden's message of October 7, 2001, began: "God Almighty hit the United States.... He destroyed its greatest buildings." Although human agents were involved, they were successful only because "Almighty God... allowed them to destroy the United States."[33] In his message of November 3, 2001, bin Laden said, "This war is fundamentally religious," being between atheists and infidels, on the one hand, and "those who believe that there is no God but Allah," on the other. He also said that if people are helped or harmed, it is always by "something that God has already preordained for [them]."[34]

By contrast, the 2004 lecture, in which the bin Laden figure set out to address "the war, its causes and consequences," provided a purely secular causal analysis, with solely human actors: Bush, al-Qaeda, and the American people. This bin Laden figure was a rationalist, saying: "One of the most important things rational people do when calamities occur is to look for their causes so as to avoid them." He even said to the American people, "Your security is in your own hands." Would a devout Wahabi Muslim not consider such a statement blasphemous? This Osama bin Laden figure would clearly seem to be an impostor—and a bad one at that.

The FBI's Apparent Skepticism: Another reason to consider this 2004 video a fake is the fact that the FBI evidently doubts its authenticity. Although its bin Laden figure confessed to planning the 9/11 attacks, in 2006 a spokesman for the FBI said, as we saw earlier, that it had no hard evidence of bin Laden's responsibility for the attacks. If the FBI had considered this videotape authentic, it probably would have regarded it as solid evidence that bin Laden had planned the attacks, so the FBI page on bin Laden as a Most Wanted Terrorist would now list 9/11 as one of his terrorist attacks.

Failure to Use English: Still another strong reason to doubt that the man on this videotape was Osama bin Laden is the fact that, although he was directly addressing the American people, he did not speak in English, in spite of bin Laden's reported facility in this language. About two weeks after 9/11, General Hamid Gul, the former head of Pakistani intelligence, said during an interview with Arnaud de Borchgrave, editor-at-large for United Press International:

> I know bin Laden and his associates. I've been with them here, in Europe and the Middle East. They are graduates of the best universities and are highly intelligent with impressive degrees and speak impeccable English.[35]

Although Gul's statement was about "bin Laden and his associates," there is no reason to doubt that bin Laden himself could speak

English well. He began studying English in the most prestigious high school in Jedda in 1968, when he was eleven years old, and he remained at this school for eight years, after which he attended a university.[36] Edward Girardet, a British journalist who met bin Laden in Afghanistan in 1989, reported that this "mysterious Arab warrior" spoke in English for 45 minutes.[37] If bin Laden spoke English impeccably, or at least reasonably well, would he not have used it when he was directly addressing the American people?

Apparently Designed to Aid Bush's Reelection: Finally, in addition to all these reasons to consider this confession video a fake, there is one more: Just as the confession video of 2001 appeared at an opportune time for the Bush administration, so did this one, showing up right before the 2004 presidential election. It is, in fact, sometimes called "the October Surprise video." As this name suggests, although the bin Laden of the video appeared to be trying to hurt Bush's chances by ridiculing and excoriating him, its rather predictable effect on the American electorate was to increase the vote for Bush—because if bin Laden was trying to get Bush defeated, many Americans would see this as a good reason to vote *for* him. In any case, it was widely accepted that any reminder of the threat from bin Laden would help Bush because of his reputation for being "tough on terrorism."

The timing of this video's appearance even led former CBS anchorman Walter Cronkite to suggest that its production may have been arranged by "Karl Rove, the political manager at the White House, who is a very clever man." Cronkite did, to be sure, accept the tape's authenticity, suggesting merely that Rove had "probably set up bin Laden to this thing."[38] But in light of the various reasons to doubt that the bearded man on the tape was really bin Laden, a more likely speculation might be that Rove had arranged for a fake video to be made.

In either case, the speculation that Rove was behind the video-tape's appearance lends interest to a comment that Rove reportedly made about the tape the day it appeared. According to Robert

Draper's book about the Bush presidency, Rove said, after an aide brought up the tape: "This has the feel of something that's not gonna hurt us at all."[39]

According to journalist Ron Suskind, CIA analysts agreed among themselves that "bin Laden's message was clearly designed to assist the President's reelection." Deputy Director John McLaughlin, according to Suskind, got "nods from CIA officers at the table" when he began a discussion of the video by saying: "Bin Laden certainly did a nice favor today for the President."[40]

If the purpose of the tape's release was to aid Bush, moreover, it was a great success, as indicated two days after its release by an article in London's *Telegraph*, which began:

> President Bush has opened a six-point lead over John Kerry in the first opinion poll to include sampling taken after the new Osama bin Laden videotape was broadcast on Friday night.
>
> The *Newsweek* poll published yesterday, only three days before the presidential election, put Mr. Bush on 50 per cent and Mr. Kerry on 44 per cent. A similar poll conducted a week earlier gave the president 48 per cent to his Democratic challenger's 46 per cent.
>
> If the trend is confirmed by other polls, Mr. Bush may have his greatest enemy to thank for helping him secure another four years in the White House after the appearance of the video sparked a sharp final round of argument over which candidate can best defeat terrorism.[41]

After the election, moreover, both Bush and Kerry reportedly believed that the video had helped Bush win.[42] Given both the timing and the effect of this video, it is appropriately called the "October Surprise" video of 2004.

To summarize: The strongest reasons for doubting the authenticity of the videotape of October 2004 are the bin Laden figure's appearance, his non-religious language and causal analysis, his failure to use English even though he was addressing the American people, and the fact that the tape, surfacing just before the presidential election, seemed designed to help assure Bush's victory. Accordingly, the videotape of October 2004 did not provide credible evidence that Osama bin Laden was still alive. It instead provided strong evidence that someone was seeking to convince us that he was still alive.

THE AUDIOTAPE OF DECEMBER 17, 2004

On December 17, 2004, a 70-minute audiotape, purportedly from Osama bin Laden, appeared on Arab websites. The speaker accused the Saudi royal family of being puppets of a Crusader–Zionist alliance and praised the December 6 attack on the US consulate in Saudi Arabia.[43]

This tape was widely taken as authentic. On PBS's *Newshour with Jim Lehrer*, for example, correspondent Spencer Michels properly noted that this new message was "allegedly from bin Laden." The program also showed Colin Powell saying that commentators should "give our intelligence communities time to… make sure it is bin Laden." But Michels then proceeded, along with Jim Lehrer himself and their guests, to discuss the new message as if there were no question about its authenticity.

Simply assuming that the tape really was from bin Laden, this program used it as an occasion to discuss the possibility of finding him. Lehrer asked Michael Scheuer, the former chief of the CIA's bin Laden unit: "Where is this guy, Osama bin Laden? Why can't anybody find him?" Scheuer said:

> Well, he's certainly on the border somewhere between
> Pakistan and Afghanistan…. He is amongst a culture
> that values perhaps more than anything protecting their
> guests.

That was Scheuer's explanation for why bin Laden had not been found. Daniel Benjamin, who had been a member of the National Security Council during the Clinton administration, agreed, adding that bin Laden had "set up an awful lot of early warning systems in the various villages among loyalists who could warn him of movements that were directed at him." The possibility that bin Laden might be dead was simply not mentioned.

This program only brought up the subject of bin Laden's possible death very indirectly, by including current footage of Pakistan's President Musharraf—who back in late 2001 and early 2002 had expressed his opinion that bin Laden was dead—saying: "I know that he is alive, but I don't know where he is." The fact that this represented a change of mind on Musharraf's part was not discussed.[44]

On CNN, Peter Bergen, who had indicated in early 2002 that bin Laden appeared to need dialysis for kidney disease, did not mention the possibility that bin Laden might be dead, nor did he otherwise question the authenticity of the new tape. He instead suggested that the rapidity with which bin Laden had issued a reply to the December 6 attack meant that he lived in a secure location. With regard to the question of why bin Laden had not been found, Bergen stated that he and his deputy Ayman al-Zawahri had released almost 30 messages since 9/11, after which Bergen said:

> [T]he chain of custody of these tapes is the one way to find bin Laden…. It's extraordinary that the chain of custody of these tapes has not been traced back. After all, they're releasing these tapes very frequently, on average once every six weeks, yet it seems that American intelligence agencies or other intelligence agencies are not capable of tracing back the source of these tapes.[45]

The possibility that the source of the "bin Laden tapes" might not have been Osama bin Laden himself, so that tracing the chain of custody back to the source might not have led to him, was not mentioned.

CNN began this program by saying that CIA officials had "a high degree of confidence" that the voice on the audiotape was bin Laden's.[46] But two years later, the BBC, in a summary of alleged bin Laden tapes, reported that the identity of the voice on this audiotape of December 2004 "cannot be confirmed."[47]

THE AUDIOTAPE OF DECEMBER 27, 2004

On December 27, 2004, which was just over a month before Iraqis were scheduled to go to the polls (on January 30, 2005), an audiotape purportedly from Osama bin Laden encouraged them to boycott the election.[48] Although the headlines of news reports at the time highlighted this as the audiotape's most significant aspect,[49] it appears likely in retrospect that the most important feature was the fact that the bin Laden voice referred to Abu Musab al-Zarqawi as the "emir" (leader) of al-Qaeda in Iraq.

The significance of this feature arises from the fact that eleven months earlier, in February 2004, *New York Times* reporter Dexter Filkins had reported the existence of a letter from al-Zarqawi to al-Qaeda leaders in Afghanistan.[50] This audiotape of December 27, 2004, could hence be taken as the response to that letter by Osama bin Laden himself, anointing al-Zarqawi as the leader of the al-Qaeda movement in Iraq.

This connection, however, provides a reason for skepticism about the audiotape's authenticity. This is because at the time the Filkins story appeared, as we will see later, the Bush administration and the Pentagon were engaged in a propaganda campaign to make al-Zarqawi appear to be a central member of al-Qaeda and a crucial figure in the Iraqi resistance to the US occupation. One dimension of this propaganda effort was the leaking of the so-called al-Zarqawi letter to Filkins. The fact that this letter was most likely fabricated by US military intelligence provides a reason to believe that the audiotape of December 27, 2004, in which the bin Laden voice designated al-Zarqawi the leader of al-Qaeda in Iraq, was also fabricated.

This audiotape, however, was generally accepted as authentic by the press. For example, a *Christian Science Monitor* article, entitled "In Iraq, a Clear-Cut Bin Laden–Zarqawi Alliance," began: "The connection between Osama bin Laden and Abu Musab al-Zarqawi was cemented with Mr. bin Laden's latest taped statement on Tuesday." The article consistently referred to the speaker simply as "bin Laden," never raising the possibility that the tape might have been a fake.[51]

A story by Agence France-Presse was more cautious. Besides putting scare quotes around "bin Laden" in its title ("'Bin Laden' Calls for Iraqi Poll Boycott"), it generally spoke of "the voice attributed to bin Laden," "the man purported to be bin Laden," or simply "the voice." It also pointed out that the tape's "authenticity could not be confirmed." However, even this story began by saying that "Al Qaeda chief Osama bin Laden has recognised Abu Musab al-Zarqawi… as leader of his terror network in Iraq," thereby implying that the tape was probably authentic.[52]

An Associated Press story was also cautious. It stated that the message was "said to be made by the terrorist leader Osama bin Laden"; it always referred to the "voice on the tape" or the "man speaking on the tape"; it added that there was "no way to confirm the speaker's identity independently"; and it even added: "In Washington, a State Department spokesman, Adam Ereli, said it had not been determined whether the speaker was Mr. bin Laden."[53] This story made clear, therefore, that there was no basis for attributing the tape's message to Osama bin Laden himself.

In sum: Despite most of the press's confidence in its authenticity, this audiotape could not be taken as good evidence that Osama bin Laden was still alive at the end of 2004.

THE AUDIOTAPE OF JANUARY 19, 2006

After a year of silence, "Osama bin Laden" began speaking out again in 2006. On January 19, an audiotape warned that more attacks on America were being planned. Citing polls showing that the American people "do not want to fight Muslims on Muslim land," it offered "a long-term truce based on just conditions." US officials, speaking as if this offer undoubtedly came from Osama bin Laden himself, rejected it. J.D. Crouch, Bush's deputy national security advisor, added that the message provided a reminder that al-Qaeda was continuing to plot against the United States and demonstrated "why we're very much on the hunt against al-Qaeda senior leadership."[54]

As shown by its title, "Bin Laden Re-emerges," a *New York Times* story expressed no doubt about the audiotape's authenticity. It began with these paragraphs:

> Breaking more than a year's silence, Osama bin Laden warned Americans in an audiotape released today that Al Qaeda was planning more attacks on the United States, but he offered a "long truce" on undefined terms. The tape was played by the Arab satellite television station Al Jazeera, and the Central Intelligence Agency verified its authenticity this afternoon.
>
> American officials said the tape's release might have been timed to assure his followers that Mr. bin Laden was alive and well days after an American bombing of a house in a Pakistani village where senior Qaeda officials were said to have been killed.

The author of this article, seemingly intent on assuring the *Times*'s readers that bin Laden was indeed still "alive and well," next stated: "Vice President Dick Cheney, asked by Fox News about the tape, said it now seemed likely that Mr. bin Laden, whom some had believed dead, was alive." The reporter then added: "Nearly all of the video and audiotapes attributed to Mr. bin Laden in the past turned out to be authentic."[55]

This reporter did not say whether these "authentic" tapes included the videotape of November 9, 2001, in which the bin Laden figure's message and appearance differed greatly from the undoubtedly authentic bin Laden videos that emerged shortly before and after it; the audiotape of November 2002, which Swiss voice experts declared probably a fake; and the presidential election videotape of 2004, in which the bin Laden figure provided a non-religious causal analysis in which events were determined by human agents, not God.

A CNN report was more circumspect. It began: "A CIA official believes an audiotaped message threatening the United States is from al Qaeda leader Osama bin Laden." It pointed out that CIA analysts had to work with a "poor-quality audiotape." And its concluding statement began, "If the CIA voice analysis proves correct..."[56]

Was the tape really from Osama bin Laden? An ABC News report on Professor Bruce Lawrence of Duke University—whose statement about the "bogus" nature of the videotape of November 9, 2001, was quoted earlier—gave Lawrence's reasons for concluding that it was not. For one thing, Lawrence pointed out, this message did not have bin Laden's normal references to the Qur'an. Lawrence also referred to the evidence that bin Laden was no longer alive[57]—a possibility that was not even mentioned by the *New York Times* or CNN, even though both organizations had in earlier years discussed it openly.

The Audiotape of April 23, 2006

After the terrorist attack in Mumbai, India, in November 2008, a "bin Laden audiotape" that had appeared on April 23, 2006, came back into the news, because its bin Laden voice had denounced a "Crusader–Zionist–Hindu war against Muslims." On December 6, 2008, a *New York Times* story, stating that "American intelligence officials are all but certain that Lashkar[-e-Taiba] led the [Mumbai] attacks," stated: "[O]n April 23, 2006, Osama bin Laden seemed to signal an open alliance with groups like Lashkar, and their goals." The evidence for this claim was the fact that the April 23 audiotape had referred to a "Crusader–Zionist–Hindu war against Muslims." This *Times* story raised no question about the authenticity of that audiotape, simply saying, for example: "Mr. bin Laden called for Islamic holy warriors to continue jihad against India over Kashmir."[58]

Back on April 24, 2006, just after that audiotape had appeared, the *New York Times* had expressed this same lack of skepticism, saying: "Osama bin Laden denounced what he called a 'Zionist-crusaders war on Islam' in an audiotape broadcast Sunday."[59]

The author of this story in the *Times* did at least raise the issue of authenticity, saying that the audiotape was "deemed authentic by American intelligence officials and terrorism experts." He even admitted that "there was no way to absolutely confirm the tape's authenticity." He added, however, that "terrorism experts said it was credible in part because it hewed closely to Mr. bin Laden's ideological and tactical profile."[60]

Evidently taking that as sufficient proof—thereby overlooking the possibility that someone fabricating a tape could have written a script reflecting "bin Laden's ideological and tactical profile"—the reporter showed in the remainder of the article that he was undeterred by the inability to say "absolutely" that the tape was authentic, repeatedly referring to the speaker as "Mr. bin Laden."

The treatment by other reporters was equally or even more superficial. Most of them simply reported that White House Press Secretary Scott McClellan, when asked about this audiotape during a press briefing, said: "I just heard from the intelligence community that they believe it is authentic."[61] A story by Reuters and the Australian Broadcasting Corporation News did show a little caution, referring to the tape's "speaker" and saying that it was "attributed to" bin Laden. By the end, however, the story simply referred to the speaker as "bin Laden" and told readers that he "has been on the run since the US campaign to oust Afghanistan's Taliban government in 2001."[62]

THE AUDIOTAPE OF JUNE 30, 2006

On June 7, 2006, Abu Musab al-Zarqawi was reportedly killed. Three weeks later, on June 30, an audiotaped message, purportedly from bin Laden, called al-Zarqawi "one of our greatest knights." The speaker also, after telling President Bush that he should have al-Zarqawi's body returned to his family, declared: "We will continue, God willing, to fight you and your allies everywhere, in Iraq, Afghanistan, Somalia and Sudan, until we drain your money and kill your men and send you home defeated, God willing, as we defeated you before, thanks to God, in Somalia." CNN reported that the CIA declared the voice on the recording to be that of bin Laden.[63]

However, as we saw above, the tape could have been a fabrication even if that was true. And, given the reasons discussed earlier to doubt the authenticity of the purported al-Zarqawi letter to al-

Qaeda of February 2004 and of the audiotape of the following December, in which the bin Laden voice designated al-Zarqawi the "emir" of al-Qaeda in Iraq, there is also good reason to doubt the authenticity of bin Laden's purported tribute to al-Zarqawi in this 2006 tape.

THE VIDEOTAPE OF JULY 14, 2007

A 50-second segment in which Osama bin Laden praised martyrdom was contained in a 40-minute video that appeared July 14, 2007. Some of the headlines about this video—such as "Bin Laden Appears in New al-Qaida Video," "Newly Released Message: Osama Bin Laden Calls for Islamic Martyrdom," and "Possible New Message from Osama bin Laden"[64]—gave the impression that it contained fresh footage of bin Laden. However, as the latter two of these three stories acknowledged, the clip of bin Laden was old, which meant that it provided no evidence that he was still alive in 2007.

THE VIDEOTAPE OF SEPTEMBER 6, 2007

On September 6, 2007—five days before the sixth anniversary of 9/11—a new "bin Laden videotape" appeared.[65] If the authenticity of the videotapes of 2001 and 2004 had been doubtful because the bin Laden figures in them appeared to have reversed the aging process, the genuineness of this one was even more suspect. In an ABC News blog entitled "New Videotape From Bin Laden; Al Qaeda's No. 1 Still Alive," which was published shortly before the videotape actually appeared, investigative reporter Brian Ross said:

> The jihadist Web site announced the tape with a banner, showing a still picture of bin Laden, now 50 years old, looking fit with a full beard of dark black hair, no gray at all.[66]

As Ross pointed out to ABC anchorman Charles Gibson during a related program, "In his [bin Laden's] last appearance, in October 2004, he had a very gray beard."[67]

However, having begun the blog by saying, "Intelligence sources tell ABC News they believe the video message from Osama bin Laden is authentic," Ross did not point out that this apparent reversal of the aging process could suggest fakery. He instead appealed to the authority of former counterterrorism coordinator Richard Clarke, who said:

> It does look oddly like he is wearing a false beard.... If we go back to the tape three years [ago], he had a very white beard. This looks like a phony beard that has been [pasted] on.[68]

So, rather than suggesting that the bin Laden figure was a fake, ABC suggested that it was the real bin Laden wearing a fake beard.

This was certainly surprising, especially in the light of Clarke's judgment that bin Laden "came up on this occasion to prove he's alive." If bin Laden wanted viewers to accept this video as truly from him, why would he have put on an obviously fake beard? Clarke's proposal was that his phony beard might mean that he was living in "southeast Asia, the Philippines, Indonesia," where "a beard would stand out," because "most men, Muslim men [there] don't have beards."[69]

But if bin Laden had shaved off his beard, why would he, after going into the studio to be videotaped, have put on a beard that was obviously phony? Are we to believe that if bin Laden was indeed living in southeast Asia, his people would not have been able to obtain a more authentic-looking beard for him?

Some reporters suggested that bin Laden may have simply dyed his beard. The Associated Press story, not allowing any peculiarities about the bin Laden figure's appearance to cast doubt on the video's authenticity and hence its evidence that bin Laden was still alive, said: "His trimmed beard is shorter than in his last video, in 2004, and is fully black—apparently dyed, since in past videos it was mostly gray.... But his appearance dispelled rumors that he had died."[70]

It is generally agreed, however, that as a devout Wahabi Muslim, the real bin Laden would not have dyed his beard.[71] In the 2008

interview quoted at the beginning of this essay, former CIA operative Robert Baer, right after saying of bin Laden, "Of course he's
dead," made an allusion to this videotape, saying: "Where are the
DVDs? Bin Laden wouldn't dye his hair."[72] Baer was thereby implying that the speaker on the videotape of September 2007 was not
bin Laden, because the real bin Laden could have had such a black
beard only by dyeing it, something he would not have done.

NBC producers Robert Windrem and Victor Limjoco discussed
this issue in a program asking, "Was Bin Laden's Last Video Faked?"
They began with this frank statement:

> When al-Qaida's media arm released its first Osama Bin
> Laden video in nearly three years, most of the media
> attention was focused on Bin Laden's beard. It appeared
> either dyed—or perhaps even pasted on. He was
> ridiculed[73] and a variety of theories were offered to
> explain it. But now, there is a running debate among
> video analysts about whether al-Qaida faked the video
> altogether.[74]

The point of departure for this debate, they explained, was
another strange thing about this video:

> [O]f the 25 minutes of video tape, only three and a half
> minutes, were moving video. The rest was covered by a
> still image or a frozen still. Moreover, the still covered
> the only time references on the 25 minute [*sic*] of tape—
> references to political developments in Iraq, Britain and
> France. This lead [*sic*] to the suspicion that the video is
> not new, but disguised to appear as new.

Windrem and Limjoco then turned to the leading proponent of this
view, Dr. Neal Krawetz, a computer consultant, who pointed out
that in most respects, this video and the "October Surprise" video
of 2004 were identical:

> Here is Bin Laden in the same clothing, same studio,
> same studio setup, and same desk *three years later*. In fact,
> his stack of papers that he reads are moved between the

exact same stacks. If you overlay the 2007 video with the
2004 video, his face has not changed in three years—
only his beard is darker.

Krawetz concluded that both videos were made on the same day.

Neither Krawetz nor the NBC producers drew the conclusion
that the man on this video was not bin Laden. The program, in fact,
quoted Krawetz as saying:

> It has been argued that the only time there are mentions
> of current events are during still frames, when Bin Laden
> is not actually moving. To suggest that he is perhaps
> dead—and this video is actually a fake—I don't think
> that you can necessarily draw that conclusion from the
> video.

In asking whether the 2007 video was faked, NBC was not asking
if the man appearing in it was not really Osama bin Laden but
merely whether an old video had been passed off as new. Addressing
this issue, Windrem and Limjoco said:

> [A] senior U.S. intelligence official tells NBC News the
> U.S. believes the tape is new. He would not discuss the
> reasons why intelligence analysts feel that way. Another
> even more senior intelligence official dismissed the possi-
> bility that that beard is fake, but would not discuss the
> reason for the darkened beard.[75]

As this statement shows, the NBC producers were clearly skeptical
of the claims by these intelligence officials.

Although they did not raise the more radical question of
fakery—whether the speaker was an impostor—their suspicion that
the video was for the most part old, having been made at the same
time as the video of October 29, 2004, is relevant to that more
radical question, because if the 2004 video was a fake, then it would
follow that this one was, too. And, as we saw above, there are very
good reasons to believe that the speaker in the 2004 video was not
Osama bin Laden.

In any case, the video of a bin Laden figure with a black beard provided no evidence that Osama bin Laden was still alive in 2007. If anything, it provided evidence to the contrary. It showed that someone had issued a bin Laden video that was a fake at least in the sense of being an old video altered to appear new.

Nevertheless, when the news media were confronted by yet another "message from bin Laden" two months later, they would for the most part treat it as still another new message from Osama bin Laden.

THE AUDIOTAPE OF NOVEMBER 2007

On November 29, 2007, Al-Jazeera played excerpts from an audio-tape entitled "Message to European Peoples." The speaker, purportedly Osama bin Laden, encouraged Europeans to tell their governments to stop assisting America with its unjust war in Afghanistan. Explaining why this war was unjust, he said:

> The events of Manhattan were retaliation against the
> American–Israeli alliance's aggression against our people
> in Palestine and Lebanon, and I am the only one respon-
> sible for it. The Afghan people and government knew
> nothing about it. America knows that.[76]

News media differed greatly on the question of the tape's authenticity.

The BBC was circumspect. The title of its report on this tape had "Bin Laden Message" in quote marks. This report spoke of the tape as "attributed to bin Laden." And, rather than ever using the phrase, "bin Laden said," this BBC report always referred to "the speaker" or "the voice."[77]

At the other end of the spectrum was the treatment by the Associated Press. Its heading said simply, "Bin Laden Urges Europe to Pull Forces from Afghanistan." Its text consistently referred to statements on the tape as having been made by bin Laden, using phrases such as "Bin Laden said" and "Bin Laden urged." The question of the tape's authenticity was not even mentioned.[78]

Most stories were somewhere between these two extremes. For

example, Reuters, after a headline and two paragraphs reporting what "bin Laden urged," referred to "a speaker in the recording who sounded like bin Laden." Reuters also reported that a US counterterrorism official said that the voice on the audiotape "appeared to be bin Laden's." After those two cautious statements, however, the story went back to reporting what "bin Laden said"—saying, for example: "bin Laden said the Taliban had no knowledge of plans for the 2001 attacks."[79]

In sum, the stories about this audiotape either treated it as authentic or assumed that, if the voice was proved to be bin Laden's, the tape could then be declared authentic (in spite of the fact that experts could have used digital manipulation to make the voice of Osama bin Laden say anything they wished). Also, none of the stories reminded readers of the evidence that bin Laden had long been dead, that none of the previous "bin Laden messages" had been fully authenticated, or that some of them quite clearly appeared to be fakes.

As to whether this audiotape should be accepted as authentic today, there is an additional reason, beyond the points just mentioned, for giving a negative judgment. This audiotape, on which the bin Laden voice confessed responsibility for 9/11, was issued back on November 19, 2007, and yet the FBI still has not added 9/11 to its list of terrorist attacks for which bin Laden is wanted. This tape also appeared less than a year before Robert Baer's poll of CIA officers, through which he learned that not one of them was certain that bin Laden was still alive. Evidently, then, neither FBI nor CIA analysts were convinced that this tape was made by Osama bin Laden himself.

THE BIN LADEN TAPES OF 2008

In 2008, new tapes purportedly from Osama bin Laden continued to appear. On March 19, the speaker on an audiotape threatened the European Union because of the reprinting of an anti-Islamic cartoon first published in Denmark in 2006.[80] The very next day, March 20, a new audiotape emerged. Saying that "Iraq is the perfect base to set up the jihad to liberate Palestine," the bin Laden voice urged people in the Middle East to liberate Gaza and support their "Mujahedeen brothers in Iraq."[81] On May 16, 2008, an audiotape with a bin Laden voice criticized Israel on the 60th anniversary of its founding and vowed to continue fighting it.[82] Two days later, on May 18, still another audiotape appeared. In this one, the bin Laden voice told Muslim militants that the only way to liberate Palestine would be to fight the Arab regimes that protect Israel. Fighting Muslim rulers is permissible, he added, if they are not governing according to Islamic law.[83]

In all of these cases, the reporters pointed out that the tapes could not be independently authenticated. It would appear, moreover, that even Vice President Cheney was not convinced of their authenticity. At the end of 2008, a reporter asked the vice president whether Osama bin Laden was still living. Cheney replied: "I don't know and I'm guessing he is."[84]

THE BIN LADEN AUDIOTAPE OF JANUARY 14, 2009

After remaining silent during the latter seven months of 2008, "Osama bin Laden" issued a new statement on January 14, 2009, just a week before the inauguration of Barack Obama as the new president of the United States. In a 22-minute audiotape titled "A Call for Jihad to Stop the Aggression on Gaza. The Message of Sheikh Osama Bin Laden to the Muslim Ummah,"[85] the voice used Israel's attack on Gaza as the occasion to issue a challenge to the future president. Saying that President-elect Obama had received a "heavy inheritance" from President Bush—two wars and the collapse of the economy—the bin Laden voice questioned whether America "is capable to keep fighting us for more years."[86]

But was the voice really that of Osama bin Laden? The BBC, exercising circumspection, announced a "new audio message purported to be from Osama Bin Laden" and consistently referred to "the speaker" and "the message," never once attributing the message to Osama bin Laden himself. Saying, "If verified, it will be the first audio tape issued by the Saudi-born militant since May

2008," the BBC added that its security correspondent says "the voice is the same." But the BBC never wrote of this tape as if the verification had taken place.[87]

However, the US press, as usual, was less cautious. The Associated Press, after saying in its first paragraph that the audiotape was "believed to carry a message from Osama bin Laden," spoke in the remainder of its story as if this belief were undoubtedly correct, attributing the statements on the tape to bin Laden himself and saying that this audiotape "was bin Laden's first since May." Unlike the BBC, the AP did not point out that this would be true only if the tape were verified.[88]

A *New York Times* article also referred to the tape as if there were no doubt about its authenticity. Titled "Bin Laden, on Tape, Urges Holy War Over Gaza," this article's first paragraph said: "Osama bin Laden exhorted Muslims to wage holy war against Israel… in an audiotape posted Wednesday on Islamist Web sites, his first public statement since May." The authors of this article did later point out that "[t]he Bin Laden tape's authenticity could not immediately be verified, but"—they immediately added, as if they were capable of carrying out this verification themselves—"it bore many hallmarks of Qaeda messages. The tape was produced by As-Sahab, the Qaeda media arm, and the voice on the tape closely resembled other recordings by Mr. bin Laden." A few paragraphs later, these journalists wrote, incongruously: "The audiotape, if verified, is the first time Mr. bin Laden has issued a public statement since May." In the preceding paragraph, however, they had written as if this verification had already taken place, following a quotation from the tape with "Mr. bin Laden said."[89]

Brian Ross of ABC News, equally willing to go beyond the evidence, used the tape as proof that rumors about bin Laden's death had been false. Saying that the tape reveals "that bin Laden is quite short of breath," Ross quoted former CIA officer John Kiriakou as referring to this tape as "the first solid evidence that there's some sort of problem with his health." What about the evidence in 2002, discussed earlier, that bin Laden was suffering from kidney disease?

Ross wrote: "In 2002, there were widespread rumors and reports that bin Laden had serious kidney problems, but U.S. officials never confirmed his diagnosis."[90]

As we saw in Chapter 1, however, these "rumors and reports" included the professional opinions of terrorist expert Peter Bergen and Dr. Sanjay Gupta, based on the post–November 9 video released December 27, 2001, that bin Laden was suffering from kidney failure, which would mean that he required a dialysis machine to stay alive, plus the testimonies of journalist Richard Labeviere and Pakistan's President Musharraf that bin Laden had ordered a mobile dialysis machine. In saying that "U.S. officials never confirmed [bin Laden's] diagnosis" in 2002, what further confirmation did Ross imagine would have been possible, short of capturing bin Laden and subjecting him to a physical examination?

In any case, addressing the question of whether the wheezing voice on this audiotape was really that of Osama bin Laden, Ross wrote: "A senior U.S. official told ABCNews.com, 'There is no reason to doubt the authenticity of the tape.'" Having used this anonymous source to settle this issue, Ross declared that the new audiotape "put an end to speculation that bin Laden could be dead." Then, almost as if to trumpet his credulity, Ross reaffirmed the authenticity of the most obviously problematic bin Laden video-tape, adding: "The last time bin Laden appeared on camera was September 2007, when he seemed to have dyed his hair and beard a dark black."[91]

To sum up this chapter: Former National Security Council member Daniel Benjamin said in late 2007: "The only proof U.S. intelligence has that bin Laden is even alive are his own videos."[92] In light of the fact that none of these videos can be considered definitely authentic, it would appear that the United States has no proof whatsoever that Osama bin Laden is still alive.

4

WHO MIGHT HAVE BEEN MOTIVATED TO
FABRICATE MESSAGES?

Besides the fact that none of the post-2001 "bin Laden tapes" are undoubtedly authentic, some of them, as we have seen, appear rather obviously to have been fakes—a fact that suggests that *all* of them may have been fabricated. These tapes have been appearing somewhat regularly since 2002. If they are fakes, the implication is that one or more organizations have been fabricating tapes to convince the world that bin Laden is still alive. Is this possible?

Technically, we have seen, it is entirely possible. The only question is whether some organization(s) with the technical ability to fabricate the tapes also had the motivation to do so.

Relevant to this question may be an article in London's *Independent* in which Nick Davies provided a preview of his book *Flat Earth News*, which is about "falsehood, distortion and propaganda in the global media."

In this article, "How the Spooks Took Over the News," Davies described "a new machinery of propaganda which has been created by the United States and its allies since the terrorist attacks of September 2001." As a result of this propaganda machinery, there is now, Davies wrote, "a concerted strategy to manipulate global perception. And the mass media are operating as its compliant assistants, failing both to resist it and to expose it."

Having mentioned America's "allies," Davies seemed to have in mind primarily the UK. After describing the Pentagon's "information operations," otherwise known as "psyops," Davies wrote: "In Britain, the Directorate of Targeting and Information Operations in the Ministry of Defence works with specialists from 15 UK psyops, based at the Defence Intelligence and Security School."[1]

One product of this propaganda machinery, Davies suggested, was the 2004 letter that was purportedly sent by Abu al-Zarqawi to al-Qaeda leaders in Afghanistan, which was mentioned in the previous chapter.

In the run-up to the invasion of Iraq, the Bush administration had portrayed al-Zarqawi, a Jordanian with at that time no connection to al-Qaeda, as the primary link between that organization and the government of Saddam Hussein. In his infamous address to the United Nations in February 2003, Secretary of State Colin Powell falsely claimed that "Iraq today harbors a deadly terrorist network headed by Abu Musab al-Zarqawi…, an associate and collaborator of Osama bin Laden."[2] Although the Bush administration never substantiated this claim, *New York Times* Baghdad correspondent Dexter Filkins was in February 2004 given access to a document, purportedly written by al-Zarqawi, that seemed to confirm, at least, that the "insurgency" in Iraq was presently being spearheaded by an al-Qaeda leader.

Filkins discussed this document and quoted it at length in a *New York Times* front-page article. Published February 9, 2004, this article began:

> American officials here [in Baghdad] have obtained a detailed proposal that they conclude was written by an operative in Iraq to senior leaders of Al Qaeda, asking for help to wage a sectarian war in Iraq in the next months. The Americans say they believe that Abu Musab al-Zarqawi, a Jordanian who has long been under scrutiny by the United States for suspected ties to Al Qaeda, wrote the undated 17-page document. Mr. Zarqawi is believed to be operating here in Iraq.

This document, Filkins reported, suggested that, although the American strategy against al-Qaeda in Iraq had been working, al-Qaeda could save itself by attacking Iraq's Shiite majority. It would thereby provoke the Shiites into attacking the Sunnis, who would then join forces with al-Qaeda.[3]

With regard to the authenticity of the document, Filkins wrote: "The American officials in Baghdad said they were confident the account was credible and said they had independently corroborated Mr. Zarqawi's authorship." Although Filkins mentioned that "other interpretations may be possible," he immediately added: "[A] senior United States intelligence official in Washington said, 'I know of no reason to believe the letter is bogus in any way.'"

Giving still more details derived from unnamed sources, Filkins wrote:

> According to the American officials here, the Arabic-language document was discovered in mid-January when a Qaeda suspect was arrested in Iraq. Under interrogation, the Americans said, the suspect identified Mr. Zarqawi as the author of the document. The man arrested was carrying it on a CD to Afghanistan, the Americans said, and intended to deliver it to people they described as the "inner circle" of Al Qaeda's leadership. That presumably refers to Osama bin Laden and his deputy, Dr. Ayman al-Zawahiri [sic].[4]

This story, which instantly became a sensation, was accepted by most of the mainstream media.[5] New York Times columnist William Safire, for example, hailed the letter discussed by Filkins as a "smoking gun," even claiming that it "demolishes the repeated claim of Bush critics that there was never a 'clear link' between Saddam and Osama bin Laden."[6]

A few reporters, however, did notice reasons to be skeptical. Writing on Newsweek's website, Christopher Dickey, the magazine's Middle East regional editor, said:

> Given the Bush administration's record peddling bad intelligence and worse innuendo, you've got to wonder if this letter is a total fake. How do we know the text is genuine? How was it obtained? By whom? And when? And how do we know it's from Zarqawi? We don't. We're expected to take the administration's word for it.[7]

Newsweek's Baghdad bureau chief, Rod Nordland, also noticed problems, saying of this document:

> [I]t's a little hard to believe in it unreservedly. It came originally from Kurdish sources who have a long history of disinformation and dissimulation. It was an electronic document on a CD-ROM, so there's no way to authenticate signature or handwriting, aside from the testimony of those captured with it, about which the authorities have not released much information.[8]

Perhaps the most telling critique came from Greg Weiher, a political scientist at the University of Houston. Writing in *Counterpunch*, Weiher pointed out that there were many reasons to doubt the letter's authenticity. For one thing, this letter, which served to confirm the Bush administration's claims, came at a time when the president's approval rating had been declining rapidly, largely because most Americans had decided that he had lied about the evidence that supposedly justified the invasion of Iraq. "[I]f you were Karl Rove, you couldn't design a better scenario to validate the administration's slant on the war than this [letter]." A second reason to be skeptical, Weiher pointed out, was the nature of the "sources" cited:

> Note the lack of citations of any specific CPA [Coalition Provisional Authority] or Bush Administration contacts. Note the lack of any confirmation of the authenticity of this letter/CD from experts or authorities aside from "U.S. officials." Note the failure to consult third-party intelligence experts, authorities on Al Qaeda, authorities on wars of national liberation. Note the failure to provide any background on the validity of claims that Zarqawi actually could have written such a letter, is still in Iraq, or collaborated with Saddam Hussein.... This story comes solely from unnamed American government sources.... Who is it that stands behind the authenticity of this document? "Senior American officials," "some American intelligence analysts,"... "two military officials."[9]

The problems pointed out by Weiher and the *Newsweek* writers should have been obvious to most reporters, but few mentioned them.

One exception was Adrian Blomfield, who wrote an article in London's *Telegraph* entitled "How US Fuelled Myth of Zarqawi the Mastermind." Quoting a military intelligence agent in Iraq as saying that Zarqawi was "more myth than man," Blomfield also said that "senior diplomats in Baghdad claim that the letter was almost certainly a hoax."[10]

The fact that the letter was probably a hoax was revealed in the US mainstream press in 2006, when Thomas Ricks wrote an exposé in the *Washington Post* entitled "Military Plays Up Role of Zarqawi." His article began:

> The U.S. military is conducting a propaganda campaign to magnify the role of the leader of al-Qaeda in Iraq, according to internal military documents and officers familiar with the program. The effort has... helped the Bush administration tie the war to the organization responsible for the Sept. 11, 2001, attacks.[11]

Drawing on a transcript of a meeting of US Army officers in the summer of 2005, Ricks quoted Colonel Derek Harvey—a military intelligence officer who had been involved in handling Iraq intelligence issues for the Joint Chiefs of Staff—as saying: "Our own focus on Zarqawi has enlarged his caricature, if you will—made him more important than he really is."

Ricks then reported on some internal military documents, saying that they referred to methods used by this propaganda campaign to—as one document put it—"Villainize Zarqawi." These methods included "media operations" and "PSYOP."

At whom were these media and psychological operations directed? Noting that it is contrary to US military policy for them to be directed at Americans, Ricks quoted Army Colonel James A. Treadwell, who in 2003 directed the US military PSYOPS unit in Iraq, as saying that this prohibition was "ingrained" in them: "You don't psyop Americans. We just don't do it."

Treadwell's assurance is, however, at odds with some recent press reports. According to the Associated Press, for example:

> [T]he Pentagon is steadily and dramatically increasing the money it spends to win what it calls "the human terrain" of world public opinion. In the process, it is raising concerns of spreading propaganda at home in violation of federal law. An Associated Press investigation found that over the past five years, the money the military spends on winning hearts and minds at home and abroad has grown by 63 percent. ... [O]n Dec. 12, the Pentagon's inspector general released an audit finding that the public affairs office may have crossed the line into propaganda. ... "They very explicitly identify American public opinion as an important battlefield," says Marc Lynch, a professor at George Washington University.[12]

This report by the Associated Press lends support to Thomas Ricks's claim about what he found, namely, that a briefing slide about US "strategic communications" in Iraq listed the "home audience" among the six major targets.

In order to reach this "home audience," did the military's propaganda campaign use American reporters? Ricks quoted Brigadier General Mark Kimmitt, who had been the military's chief spokesman when the propaganda campaign began in 2004, as saying: "We trusted Dexter [Filkins] to write an accurate story, and we gave him a good scoop.... There was no attempt to manipulate the press." Ricks, however, said that the briefings indicated otherwise:

> [T]here were direct military efforts to use the U.S. media to affect views of the war. One slide..., for example, noted that a "selective leak" about Zarqawi was made to Dexter Filkins, a *New York Times* reporter based in Baghdad.

Underscoring the significance of this discovery, Ricks wrote: "Official evidence of a propaganda operation using an American reporter is rare." Ricks also quoted Kimmitt as saying, during an internal briefing: "The Zarqawi PSYOP program is the most successful information campaign to date."[13]

Kimmitt himself evidently played a public role in this, saying on the day that Filkins's *New York Times* article appeared: "We believe the report and the document is credible, and we take the report seriously.... It is clearly a plan on the part of outsiders to come in to this country and spark civil war."[14]

It appears, therefore, that the "al-Zarqawi document" was fabricated as part of a PSYOPS campaign directed in part at the American public. The aim was to bolster support for the US military effort in Iraq by portraying it as part of the US response to 9/11.

This conclusion is relevant to the question with which we began this chapter: If fake bin Laden audiotapes and videotapes have been made to convince people that bin Laden is still alive, who might have been motivated to do this? A possible answer could be inferred from the fact that the continuation of the US military effort in Afghanistan has been closely connected to the "hunt for bin Laden." If the American public were to become convinced that bin Laden is dead, support for this effort would surely dry up. If military intelligence fabricated evidence to tie the war in Iraq to the group believed to have attacked America on 9/11, would it not have been equally motivated to fabricate evidence to support the belief that bin Laden is still alive, so that the "hunt" for him could continue?

Thanks to digital morphing, moreover, military intelligence would certainly have had the ability. Writing in 1999, as we saw, William Arkin pointed out that this technology had "come of age," being "available for use in psychological operations. PSYOPS, as the military calls it."[15]

The military also would have had the support of the Bush administration to carry out to such an operation. In February 2009, Tom Curley, the president and chief executive of the Associated Press, reported that, in the words of reporter John Hanna, "[t]he Bush administration turned the U.S. military into a global propaganda machine."[16] And an Associated Press story gave this report:

Spending on public affairs has more than doubled since 2003. .... The fastest-growing part of the military media is "psychological operations," where spending has doubled since 2003.[17]

5

THE CONVENIENT TIMING OF MANY OF THE MESSAGES

One reason to consider all of the post-2001 bin Laden tapes fabrications, as we have seen, is the strong evidence that Osama bin Laden died in December 2001. A reason to suspect that these tapes have been produced by agents of the US government or its allies—rather than by its enemies—is that they and other supposed al-Qaeda messages often appeared at times that were convenient for the Bush administration: when they would boost the president's ratings or support a claim made by his administration or that of its chief ally in the "war on terror," British Prime Minister Tony Blair. The following summary serves to emphasize the regularity with which convenient messages appeared:

(1) The reporting of a "bin Laden confession video" by the *Telegraph* on November 11, 2001, and by Tony Blair three days later, as we saw in Chapter 2, came roughly a month after Blair had failed to provide convincing evidence of bin Laden's responsibility for 9/11. This reporting also occurred just as Blair's government was preparing to announce emergency powers to round up suspected terrorists—powers that would require exemption from human rights legislation.

(2) The bin Laden confession tape dated November 9, 2001, was released on December 13, 2001. Besides being a time when the Bush and Blair administrations had still failed to prove bin Laden's responsibility for 9/11, this was also a time during which a Bush administration public relations campaign was trying, as the *Washington Post* reported, "to win international public support, particularly in the Islamic world, for the anti-terrorist campaign."[1]

Another possibly relevant fact is that December 13, 2001, was approximately when bin Laden evidently died, so that stories reporting this death might have been anticipated.

(3) On September 10, 2002, the world learned of a new "bin Laden video," in which the speaker praised the nineteen men said to have hijacked the airliners involved in the 9/11 attacks. Besides coming at a time when "[m]any in the Arab and Muslim world still question[ed] whether Bin Laden was involved [in the 9/11 attacks],"[2] this video appeared just before the first anniversary of the attacks, when the world's attention was again focused on them. News reports of this tape told the public that "Al-Qaida formally claimed responsibility [in it] for the September 11 attacks"[3] and that "it left no doubt that al Qaeda was behind the terror attacks."[4]

(4) On October 27, 2002, a story filed from Afghanistan claimed that US spy satellites had intercepted a telephone call between Osama bin Laden and Mullah Omar. Headed "Bin Laden Still Alive," this story came at a time when there had been "growing speculation that bin Laden [was] dead." An unnamed senior Afghan intelligence officer was quoted as saying: "It shows [Osama bin Laden] was alive recently at least. Some people might like to think he is dead, but that's just wishful thinking."[5]

(5) Shortly over a month later—on November 12, 2002—an audiotape appeared in which a bin Laden voice referred to some recent attacks. A *New York Times* story said that this tape "apparently end[ed] months of debate in the government over whether the elusive terrorist leader is still alive."[6] (As we saw in Chapter 1, moreover, the discussion in the press about the possibility that bin Laden might be dead did largely come to an end at that time.)

(6) On February 11, 2003, as the United States was preparing to attack Iraq, an audiotape appeared in which a bin Laden voice encouraged Iraqis "to fight any US led attack on Iraq."[7] Coming on

the very day that Secretary of State Colin Powell was on Capitol Hill, making the Bush administration's case for the attack, this tape allowed Powell and the White House to claim that there was an "alliance" between bin Laden and Iraq, thereby making an attack on Iraq appear to be a justified response to 9/11.

(7) On October 29, 2004, just four days before the US presidential election, another "confession video" appeared. Its bin Laden figure delivered a message that, according to CIA analysts, was "clearly designed to assist the President's reelection."[8] And it did.

(8) The audiotape of December 27, 2004, in which the bin Laden voice referred to Abu Musab al-Zarqawi as the "emir" (leader) of al-Qaeda in Iraq, came in the midst of a US propaganda campaign to convince the American public that al-Zarqawi was connected to al-Qaeda and was a major influence in the resistance to the US occupation of Iraq. This videotape was apparently intended to be understood as bin Laden's response to the letter allegedly written by al-Zarqawi to al-Qaeda leaders in Afghanistan (which was later revealed to be a hoax).

(9) To mention now a couple of tapes not previously discussed: On January 30, 2006, a videotape apparently of Osama bin Laden's deputy, Ayman al-Zawahri, was broadcast by Al-Jazeera. Besides berating Bush as a "failure" and a "butcher," the al-Zawahri figure threatened further attacks on the United States.[9] A 2004 study had shown that such threats had consistently raised the president's approval ratings,[10] and this one came the day before President Bush's State of the Union address.

(10) On May 23, 2006, an audiotape was released in which a bin Laden voice used the conviction earlier that month of Zacarias Moussaoui, the so-called twentieth hijacker, as the occasion to confess responsibility for the 9/11 attacks, saying: "I am the one in charge of the 19 brothers, and I never assigned brother Zacarias to

be with them in that mission."[11] The timing of this tape was significant because it came shortly after the publication of a Zogby poll showing that 45 percent of the US population thought the 9/11 attacks should be reinvestigated, with 42 percent believing that the US government and the 9/11 Commission had concealed "critical evidence that contradicts their official explanation of the September 11th attacks."[12] Although this timing could have been merely coincidental, the same sequence occurred again the following year (see point 11, below).

(11) September 6, 2007, brought the appearance of the video with the black-bearded bin Laden figure, who criticized both capitalism and President Bush. The timing of this video gave Bush the opportunity to say, just five days before the sixth anniversary of 9/11, that it was "a reminder about the dangerous world in which we live" and also a reminder of the importance of showing "resolve and determination to protect ourselves, deny al-Qaeda safe haven[,] and support young democracies."[16] A perhaps even more significant fact was that this video appeared the same day as the results of a new Zogby poll, which showed that 51 percent of Americans wanted a congressional investigation of the actions of Bush and Cheney in relation to 9/11.[17]

In sum, the timing of these messages suggests that they were produced by supporters, not enemies, of the Bush administration. As to why, Robert Baer has recently said: "I believe there's a vast industry of contractors, corporations, and pundits who need bin Laden alive, all of them eating at the trough."[18]

Summary and Conclusion

Much evidence, as we have seen, points to the conclusion that Osama bin Laden is no longer alive. This evidence includes the following points:

· A Pakistani newspaper published a report that a funeral ceremony for bin Laden occurred on December 15, 2001.

· The likelihood that bin Laden had died shortly before December 15 was increased by the fact that no messages from him have been intercepted by US intelligence since about December 13, 2001.

· The likelihood that bin Laden had died was also increased by credible reports that he had been suffering from kidney disease and that, when he made his final undoubtedly authentic videotape sometime after November 16, he appeared to be seriously ill (as pointed out by Peter Bergen and Dr. Sanjay Gupta).

· President Bush, Secretary of Defense Rumsfeld, and Kenton Keith (the spokesman for the US-led coalition in Afghanistan) all suggested in late 2001 or early 2002 that bin Laden might be dead. Vice President Cheney expressed the same thought at the end of 2008.

· Several people with access to inside information—including Robert Baer, Bruce Lawrence, Oliver North, Dale Watson, and sources within Israeli intelligence—expressed their strong belief that bin Laden was no longer alive.

· At one time or another, several mainstream news organizations—including the Associated Press, CBS News, CNN, Fox News, the *New York Times,* the *Telegraph*, and *Time* magazine—put out stories suggesting that bin Laden had died.

· It is widely agreed that the post-2001 "messages from bin Laden" provide the only evidence that he was still alive after 2001, but none of these can be considered definitely authentic.

· Some of the post-2001 audiotapes and videotapes purportedly from bin Laden seem rather clearly to have been fabricated, which suggests that all of them likely were.

· Many of the tapes purportedly from bin Laden and other al-Qaeda figures have appeared at times that were very convenient from the viewpoint of the Bush administration, which suggests that they were being issued by its friends rather than its enemies.

· In 2008, a Western intelligence analyst said that the cessation of intelligence information about Osama bin Laden in December 2001 had been permanent: "We have had *no* credible intelligence on OBL since 2001. All the rest is rumor and rubbish either whipped up by the media or churned out in the power corridors of western capitals."[1] The absence of any intelligence about bin Laden whatsoever—given spy satellites and the $25 million reward offered for information about him—provides further reason to conclude that he is no longer with us.

The available evidence, therefore, supports Robert Baer's statement, made in October 2008, that Osama bin Laden is dead.

If that is correct, then Baer's conclusion about the "hunt for bin Laden" follows: "This could be an eternal war if the goal is to capture this man dead or alive."[2]

It may be, of course, that a desire by certain parties for just such a war has provided the motivation to create fake bin Laden messages.

Notes

INTRODUCTION

1. Robert Baer, *See No Evil: The True Story of a Ground Soldier in the CIA's War on Terrorism* (New York: Crown, 2002).

2. "Ex-CIA Operative Discusses 'The Devil We Know,'" Interview with Terry Gross on *Fresh Air*, WHYY, 2 October 2008 (www.npr.org/templates/story/story.php?storyId=95285396).

3. "Report: Bin Laden May Be Planning Large Scale Terror Attack Against U.S.," National Terror Alert Response Center, 10 November 2008 (www.nationalterroralert.com/updates/2008/11/10/report-bin-laden-may-be-planning-large-scale-terror-attack-against-us).

4. See Paola Totaro, "Bin Laden 'Plans New Attack on US,'" *Sydney Morning Herald* 10 November 2008 (www.smh.com.au/news/world/bin-laden-plans-new-attack-on-us/2008/11/10/1226165435339.html), which was based on a story in *Al-Quds al-Arabi*, an Arabic newspaper published in London.

5. Karen DeYoung, "Obama to Explore New Approach in Afghanistan War," *Washington Post* 11 November 2008 (www.washingtonpost.com/wp-dyn/content/article/2008/11/10/AR2008111002897_pf.html).

6 Angelo M. Codevilla, "Osama bin Elvis," *American Spectator*, March 2009 (spectator.org/archives/2009/03/13/osama-bin-elvis/print).

CHAPTER 1: EVIDENCE THAT OSAMA BIN LADEN IS DEAD

1. "Translation of Funeral Article in Egyptian Paper" (www.welfarestate.com/binladen/funeral). This story was also reported by the United News of India (UNI) entitled "Osama Died a Natural Death, Buried: Taliban," ExpressIndia.com, 25 December 2001 (www.expressindia.com/news/fullstory.php?newsid=5859).

2. In "Muslim Customs Surrounding Death, Bereavement, Postmortem Examinations, and Organ Transplants," A. R. Gatrad says: "It is a religious requirement that the body be ritually washed and draped before burial, which should be as soon as possible after death," *British Medical Journal* 309 (20 August 1994): 521–523 (www.bmj.com/cgi/content/extract/309/6953/521). Also see "Islam Burial Rituals and Practices" (studentwebs.coloradocollege.edu/~l_jenkins/islam.htm): "In the Islam religion, it is customary to begin processes for burying the dead within 24 hours of the death"; and Huda, "Islamic Funeral Rites," About.com (islam.about.com/cs/elderly/a/funerals.htm), which says: "Muslims strive to bury the deceased as soon as possible after death, avoiding the need for embalming or otherwise disturbing the body of the deceased."

3. "Report: Bin Laden Already Dead," Fox News, 26 December 2001 (www.foxnews.com/story/0,2933,41576,00.html).

4. For a photo from the video, see "Transcript: Bin Laden Video Excerpts," BBC News, 27 December 2001 (news.bbc.co.uk/2/hi/middle_east/1729882.stm).

5. Toby Harnden, "US Casts Doubt on Bin Laden's Latest Message," *Telegraph* 27 December 2001 (www.telegraph.co.uk/news/worldnews/asia/afghanistan/1366508/US-casts-doubt-on-bin-Laden%27s-latest-message.html).

6. Ibid.

7. Ibid.

8. Ibid. Bin Laden also said that it was made "three months after the September 11 attacks." If it was indeed made about December 11, that would mean that the bombing of the mosque at Khost, said by bin Laden to have occurred "a few days ago," would have occurred about 25 days earlier. Again, however, all we can know for sure is that it was made some time between November 16 and December 27.

9. Ibid.

10. "Secretary Rumsfeld Meeting with Troops in Kyrgyzstan," Department of Defense, 26 April 2002 (www.defenselink.mil/transcripts/transcript.aspx?transcriptid=3414).

11. "U.S. Ignores bin Laden Death Reports, Continues Search," NewsMax.com, 26 December 2001 (www.newsmax.com/archives/articles/2001/12/25/190519.shtml).

12. Ibid.

13. "Musharraf: Bin Laden Likely Dead," CNN, 19 January 2002 (archives.cnn.com/2002/WORLD/asiapcf/south/01/19/gen.musharraf.binladen.1.19/index.html).

14. Ibid.

15. "Dr. Sanjay Gupta: Bin Laden Would Need Help if on Dialysis," CNN, 21 January 2002 (www.cnn.com/2002/HEALTH/01/21/gupta.otsc/index.html). For the tape, see "Osama Bin Laden Tape Dezember [sic] 2001" (www.myvideo.de/watch/3760193/Osama_Bin_Laden_Tape_Dezember_2001).

16. "Peter Bergen: Bin Laden Has Aged 'Enormously,'" CNN, 1 February 2002 (archives.cnn.com/2002/US/02/01/gen.bergen.cnna/index.html).

17. Alexandra Richard, "CIA Agent Allegedly Met Bin Laden in July," *Le Figaro* 1 November 2001, trans. Tiphaine Dickson (www.geocities.com/johnathanrgalt/LeFigaro.html).

18. "Report: Bin Laden Treated at US Hospital," United Press International, 31 October 2001 (www.geocities.com/vonchloride/reportbinladentreatedatushospital—thewashingtontimes.html?200823).

19. Anthony Sampson, "CIA Agent Alleged to Have Met Bin Laden in

July: French Report Claims Terrorist Leader Stayed in Dubai Hospital," *Guardian* 1 November 2001 (www.guardian.co.uk/world/2001/nov/01/ afghanistan.terrorism).

20. Adam Sage, "Ailing bin Laden 'Treated for Kidney Disease,'" *London Times* 1 November 2001 (www.unansweredquestions.org/timeline/ 2001/londontimes110101.html).

21. Romesh Ratnesar, "Osama bin Laden: Dead or Alive?" *Time* 23 June 2002 (www.time.com/time/magazine/article/0,9171,265412,00.html).

22. "FBI Official Thinks Bin Laden Is Dead," CBS News, 17 July 2002 (www.cbsnews.com/stories/2002/07/17/attack/main515468.shtml).

23. Amir Taheri, "The Death of bin Ladenism," *New York Times* 11 July 2002 (query.nytimes.com/gst/ fullpage.html?res=9405EFDE1230F932A25754C0A9649C8B63).

24. Kelli Arena and Barbara Starr, "Sources: No Bodyguards, No bin Laden," CNN, 30 July 2002 (www.cnn.com/2002/US/07/30/binladen.son).

25. Philip Shenon, "Oliver North Tells a Tall Tale of White House Intrigue," *New York Times* 27 August 2002 (query.nytimes.com/gst/ fullpage.html?res=9C06E5DC113CF934A1575BC0A9649C8B63).

26. "Karzai: Bin Laden 'Probably' Dead," CNN, 7 October 2002 (edition.cnn.com/2002/WORLD/asiapcf/central/10/06/karzai.binladen).

27. "Israeli Intelligence: Bin Laden is Dead, Heir Has Been Chosen," *World Tribune* 16 October 2002 (www.worldtribune.com/worldtribune/ WTARC/2002/me_terrorism_10_16.html).

28. "Pakistani Paper: Bin Laden Is Dead," ArabicNews.com, 26 October 2002 (www.arabicnews.com/ansub/Daily/Day/021026/2002102602.html).

29. "Rumsfeld Mixes Up Hussein, Bin Laden in Speech," *Los Angeles Times* 11 September 2004 (articles.latimes.com/2004/sep/11/world/fg-rummy11). As the title of this article indicates, Rumsfeld actually said "Saddam Hussein." It was clear, however, that he was referring to Osama bin Laden.

30. "Secretary Rumsfeld Interview with Fox's Rita Cosby," Department of Defense, 29 September 2004 (www.defenselink.mil/transcripts/ transcript.aspx?transcriptid=2438).

31. Declan Walsh, "The Hunt," *Guardian* 11 September 2006 (www.guardian.co.uk/world/2006/sep/11/afghanistan.usa).

32. "Ex-CIA Operative Discusses 'The Devil We Know,'" Interview with Terry Gross on *Fresh Air*, WHYY, 2 October 2008 (www.npr.org/templates/story/story.php?storyId=95285396).

33. Robert Baer, "When Will Obama Give Up the Bin Laden Ghost Hunt?" *Time* 18 November 2008 (www.time.com/time/world/ article/0,8599,1859354,00.html).

34 Angelo M. Codevilla, "Osama bin Elvis," *American Spectator*, March 2009 (spectator.org/archives/2009/03/13/osama-bin-elvis/print). Codevilla,

citing one piece of evidence that I do not employ, wrote: "Benazir Bhutto—as well connected as anyone with sources of information on the Afghan–Pakistani border—mentioned casually in a BBC interview that Osama had been murdered by his associates." Codevilla was referring to the fact that Bhutto, the former Pakistani prime minister, while being interviewed by David Frost on November 2, 2007, had referred in passing to Omar Sheikh as "the man who murdered Osama bin Laden?" (see "Frost over the World—Benazir Bhutto—02 Nov 07" [www.youtube.com/watch?v=oIO8B6fpFSQ]). This statement has widely been taken as good evidence that bin Laden is dead. However, Bhutto most likely simply misspoke. Omar Sheikh is widely known as the man who murdered Daniel Pearl. Shortly before making her statement, moreover, she had referred to one of the sons of Osama bin Laden, so she had his name on her mind. She almost certainly meant to say, "Omar Sheikh, the man murdered Daniel Pearl." That she did not mean to say "Osama bin Laden" is shown by the fact that, while speaking to CNN the very next day, she said: "I don't think General Musharaf personally knows where Osama bin Laden is." And then ten days later, speaking to NPR, she reported having asked a policeman assigned to guard her house: "Shouldn't you be looking for Osama bin Laden?" All of this is explained and documented in an excellent YouTube video, "Bhutto Didn't Mean to Say 'Osama bin Laden'" (www.youtube.com/watch?v=2IIn_UnLO9I&feature=related).

35. "Israeli Intelligence: Bin Laden is Dead, Heir Has Been Chosen."

CHAPTER 2: TWO FAKE BIN LADEN VIDEOS IN 2001?

1. David Bamber, "Bin Laden: Yes, I Did It," *Telegraph* 11 November 2001 (www.telegraph.co.uk/news/worldnews/asia/afghanistan/1362113/Bin-Laden-Yes,-I-did-it.html).

2. Ibid.

3. "UK Offers New Bin Laden Evidence," CNN, 14 November 2001 (archives.cnn.com/2001/WORLD/europe/11/14/inv.britain.proof/index.html).

4. T.R. Reid, "Blair Reveals Evidence Against Bin Laden: On Video, Bin Laden Says Al Qaeda 'Instigated' Sept. 11 Attacks," *Washington Post* 14 November 2001 (www.washingtonpost.com/ac2/wp-dyn/A29666-2001Nov14).

5. Secretary of State Colin Powell made this promise on NBC's *Meet the Press*, 23 September 2001 (www.washingtonpost.com/wp-srv/nation/specials/attacked/transcripts/nbctext092301.html). The promise was withdrawn the next morning in a joint press conference with President Bush, as can be seen in "Remarks by the President, Secretary of the Treasury O'Neill and Secretary of State Powell on Executive Order," White House, 24 September 2001 (www.whitehouse.gov/news/releases/2001/09/20010924-4.html).

6. "Responsibility for the Terrorist Atrocities in the United States," Office

of the Prime Minister, 4 October 2001 (news.bbc.co.uk/2/hi/uk_news/politics/1579043.stm).

7. Ibid., point 62 and opening statement.

8. "The Investigation and the Evidence," BBC News, 5 October 2001 (news.bbc.co.uk/2/hi/americas/1581063.stm).

9. "Bin Laden 'Hidden by Taleban,'" BBC News, 30 September 2001 (news.bbc.co.uk/2/hi/middle_east/1571689.stm).

10. Reid, "Blair Reveals Evidence Against Bin Laden."

11. David Bamber, "Bin Laden: Yes, I Did It."

12. "U.S. Releases Videotape of Osama bin Laden," Department of Defense, 13 December 2001 (www.defenselink.mil/releases/release.aspx?releaseid=3184); "Pentagon Releases Bin Laden Videotape: U.S. Officials Say Tape Links Him to Sept. 11 Attacks," National Public Radio, 13 December 2001 (www.npr.org/news/specials/response/investigation/011213.binladen.tape.html). The entire video can be viewed at this NPR webpage.

13. Walter Pincus and Karen DeYoung, "U.S. Says New Tape Points to Bin Laden," *Washington Post* 9 December 2001 (www.washingtonpost.com/wp-dyn/content/article/2007/11/18/AR2007111800690.html).

14. "Bush: Tape Will Show Bin Laden Is Guilty," CNN, 10 December 2001 (archives.cnn.com/2001/US/12/10/gen.war.against.terror/index.html).

15. "UK Talks on Afghan Troops," BBC News, 14 December 2001 (news.bbc.co.uk/2/hi/uk_news/1709867.stm).

16. "Tape 'Proves Bin Laden's Guilt,'" BBC News, 14 December 2001 (news.bbc.co.uk/2/hi/south_asia/1708091.stm).

17. "In His Own Words," *Newshour with Jim Lehrer* transcript, PBS *Online NewsHour*, 13 December 2001 (www.pbs.org/newshour/bb/terrorism/july-dec01/video.html).

18. Transcript of 9 November 2001 bin Laden video (www.pbs.org/newshour/terrorism/international/video_12-13.html).

19. "Could the Bin Laden Video Be a Fake?" BBC News, 14 December 2001 (news.bbc.co.uk/2/hi/1711288.stm).

20. "'Feeble' to Claim Bin Laden Tape Fake: Bush," CBC, 14 December 2001 (www.cbc.ca/world/story/2001/12/14/bush_osama011214.html).

21. Steven Morris, "US Urged to Detail Origin of Tape," *Guardian* 15 December 2001 (www.guardian.co.uk/world/2001/dec/15/september11.afghanistan).

22. "UK Talks on Afghan Troops."

23. "'Feeble' to Claim Bin Laden Tape Fake: Bush."

24. Morris, "US Urged to Detail Origin of Tape."

25. "Could the Bin Laden Video Be a Fake?"

26. "US Urged to Detail Origin of Tape."

27. "Could the Bin Laden Video Be a Fake?"

28. See the transcript of the 9 November 2001 video at PBS (www.pbs.org/newshour/terrorism/international/video_12-13.html). For a humorous example in which an authentic tape of Osama bin Laden has been morphed to make him appear to be speaking English, see "Osama Bin Laden Death Video" (www.youtube.com/watch?v=s2tcK6XPqbI&feature=related).

29. "Tape 'Proves Bin Laden's Guilt.'"

30. Pincus and DeYoung, "U.S. Says New Tape Points to Bin Laden."

31. Ibid.

32. "Bin Laden Denies Being Behind Attacks," Associated Press, 16 September 2001 (www2.jsonline.com/news/nat/sep01/binladen-denial.asp).

33. "Pakistan to Demand Handover of Bin Laden," *Guardian* 16 September 2001 (www.guardian.co.uk/world/2001/sep/16/september11.usa16).

34. "Interview with Usama bin Laden," *Ummat* (Karachi), 28 September 2001 (www.ilaam.net/Sept11/OBLInterview.html). Bin Laden's statement about innocents repeated what he had said in an interview with John Miller of ABC News in 1998: "Our religion forbids us from killing innocent people such as women and children" (web.archive.org/web/20010927151820/ http://abcnews.go.com/sections/world/DailyNews/miller_binladen_980609.html).

35. "Bin Laden's Message to the US," *Asia Times* 10 October 2001 (www.atimes.com/media/CJ10Ce02.html); the text of the speech can be read at "Osama bin Laden Speeches," September 11 News.com (www.september11news.com/OsamaSpeeches.htm).

36. "Osama bin Laden Speeches" (see previous note).

37. For a photograph from the 7 October 2001 video, see "Bin Laden Defiant," BBC, 7 October 2001 (news.bbc.co.uk/2/hi/south_asia/ 1585501.stm), or Mark Tran, "Bin Laden Makes Defiant TV Appearance," *Guardian* 7 October 2001 (www.guardian.co.uk/world/2001/oct/07/afghanistan.terrorism13).

38. For a photograph from the video of 3 November 2001, see "Bin Laden Lashes Out at U.N., U.S. Attacks in Taped Message," CNN, 3 November 2001 (archives.cnn.com/2001/WORLD/asiapcf/central/ 11/03/ret.bin.laden.statement/index.html). Bin Laden's appearance in the October 7 and November 3 videos can also be seen in "Osama bin Laden Speeches," September 11 News.com (www.september11news.com/ OsamaSpeeches.htm).

39. For a photograph from the post–November 16 video, which was aired 27 December 2001, see either "Osama bin Laden Speeches" or "Transcript: Bin Laden Video Excerpts," BBC News, 27 December 2001 (news.bbc.co.uk/ 2/hi/middle_east/1729882.stm). A portion of the November 9 video is on YouTube (www.youtube.com/watch?v=x0FVeqCX6z8).

40. For a nose comparison, see "Osama bin Laden Gets a Nose Job" (www.awitness.org/news/december_2001/osama_nose_job.html) or "Bruce

Lawrence," Radio Du Jour (www.radiodujour.com/people/lawrence_bruce).

41. Compare this man's hands with bin Laden's hand as shown in the post–November 16 video (news.bbc.co.uk/2/hi/middle_east/1729882.stm).

42. This can be seen in a portion of the November 9 video placed on YouTube (www.youtube.com/watch?v=x0FVeqCX6z8).

43. "Transcript of Usama bin Laden Video Tape," Department of Defense, 13 December 2001 (www.defenselink.mil/news/Dec2001/d20011213ubl.pdf).

44. For the government documentation of these ticket purchases, see the "Complete 9/11 Timeline" at History Commons, "August 25–September 5, 2001: Hijackers Spend Over $30,000 on 9/11 Tickets" (www.historycommons.org/context.jsp?item=a082401buyingtickets&scale=0).

45. "Bin Laden 'Voice' Lists Hijackers," BBC, 10 September 2002 (news.bbc.co.uk/2/hi/middle_east/2249984.stm).

46. These points were made in the testimonies of Cofer Black, Dale Watson, and Robert Mueller, 26 September 2002. See "Complete 9/11 Timeline, April 23–June 29, 2001: 9/11 'Muscle' Hijackers Arrive in US at This Time or Earlier" (www.historycommons.org/context.jsp?item=a042301muscle&scale=0).

47. "Transcript of Usama bin Laden Video Tape."

48. Pincus and DeYoung, "U.S. Says New Tape Points to Bin Laden."

49. Ibid.

50. "Tape 'Proves Bin Laden's Guilt.'"

51. "Most Wanted Terrorists: Usama bin Laden," Federal Bureau of Investigation (www.fbi.gov/wanted/terrorists/terbinladen.htm).

52. Ed Haas, "FBI says, 'No Hard Evidence Connecting Bin Laden to 9/11,'" *Muckraker Report* 6 June 2006 (www.teamliberty.net/id267.html). According to Haas (email letter of 18 August 2007), Claire Brown, editor of the *INN World Report*, told Hass that, before airing her own report about this conversation (muckrakerreport.com/sitebuildercontent/sitebuilderfiles/bin_laden_fbi.mov), she called Tomb to confirm the accuracy of the statement Haas had attributed to him. After she read it to him, she reported, Tomb said: "That's exactly what I told Mr. Haas."

53. Haas, "FBI says, 'No Hard Evidence Connecting Bin Laden to 9/11.'" After this story started flying around the Internet and was even covered by a TV station (KSLA 12 in Shreveport, Louisiana; see "Bin Laden's FBI Poster Omits Any 9/11 Connection" [http://video.google.com/videoplay?docid=-6443576002087829136]), Dan Eggen of the *Washington Post* tried to downplay its significance in an article entitled "Bin Laden, Most Wanted For Embassy Bombings?" (*Washington Post*, 28 August 2006 [www.washingtonpost.com/wp-dyn/content/article/2006/08/27/AR2006082700687.html]). Complaining about "conspiracy theorists" who claimed that "the lack of a Sept. 11 reference [on the FBI's "Most Wanted" webpage for bin Laden] suggests

that the connection to al-Qaeda is uncertain," Eggen quoted a former US attorney as explaining that the FBI could not appropriately "put up a wanted picture where no formal charges had been filed." As Rex Tomb's statement showed, however, the whole issue is why the Department of Justice has *not* formally charged bin Laden with the 9/11 attacks, and Tomb's answer was that the FBI had no hard evidence to support such a charge.

54. Lawrence is the editor of *Messages to the World: The Statements of Osama bin Laden* (London and New York: Verso, 2005).

55. Lawrence made these statements on 16 February 2007, during a radio interview conducted by Kevin Barrett of the University of Wisconsin at Madison. It can be heard at Radio Du Jour (www.radiodujour.com/people/lawrence_bruce).

56. Ibid.

Chapter 3: Purported bin Laden Messages after 2001

1. "Paper 'Receives Bin Laden E-mail,'" BBC News, 28 March 2002 (news.bbc.co.uk/hi/english/world/south_asia/newsid_1898000/1898624.stm).

2. Maamoun Youssef, "Bin Laden Alive, Promises New Attacks and TV Address, Says Al-Qaida Spokesman," Associated Press, 23 June 2002 (www2.ljworld.com/news/2002/jun/23/bin_laden_alive2).

3. "Al Jazeera: Bin Laden Tape Praises Hijackers," CNN, 9 September 2002 (archives.cnn.com/2002/WORLD/meast/09/09/binladen.tape).

4. Brian Whitaker, "Bin Laden Voice on Video, Says TV Channel," *Guardian* 10 September 2002 (www.guardian.co.uk/media/2002/sep/10/alqaida.september112001).

5. "Bin Laden 'Voice' Lists Hijackers," BBC News, 10 September 2002 (news.bbc.co.uk/2/hi/middle_east/2249984.stm).

6. Jason Burke, "Bin Laden Still Alive, Reveals Spy Satellite," *Guardian* 6 October 2002 (www.guardian.co.uk/world/2002/oct/06/alqaida.terrorism).

7. Ibid.

8. "Karzai: Bin Laden 'Probably' Dead," CNN, 7 October 2002 (edition.cnn.com/2002/WORLD/asiapcf/central/10/06/karzai.binladen).

9. Brian Whitaker, "Swiss Scientists 95% Sure that Bin Laden Recording Was a Fake," *Guardian* 30 November 2001 (www.guardian.co.uk/world/2002/nov/30/alqaida.terrorism).

10. James Risen, "Qaeda Broadcast; Experts Conclude That Voice on Tape Belongs to bin Laden," *New York Times* 19 November 2002 (query.nytimes.com/gst/fullpage.html?res=9D05E1DD1E30F93AA25752C1A9649C8B63).

11. Ibid.

12. Johanna McGeary and Douglas Waller, "Why Can't We Find Bin Laden?" *Time* 25 November 2002 (www.time.com/time/magazine/

article/0,9171,1003727,00.html).

13. Whitaker, "Swiss Scientists 95% Sure that Bin Laden Recording Was a Fake."

14. "Bin Laden Tape a Fake, Swiss Lab Says," Associated Press, 28 November 2002 (www.stopnwo.com/docs/bin_laden_tape_a_fake_swiss_lab_says.pdf).

15. "IDIAP Analysis of the Latest Bin Laden Tape," December 2002 (www.idiap.ch/pages/press/bin-laden-eval.pdf).

16. Steve Kettmann, "Doubt Cast on bin Laden Tape," Wired.com, 3 December 2002 (www.wired.com/science/discoveries/news/2002/12/56670).

17. "Tape Urges Muslim Fight against U.S.," CNN, 12 February 2003 (www.cnn.com/2003/ALLPOLITICS/02/11/powell.binladen).

18. "White House Publicizes Tape Hours Before Release," Associated Press, 11 February 2003 (www.foxnews.com/story/0,2933,78311,00.html).

19. David Johnston, "Threats and Responses: Washington, Top U.S. Officials Press Case Linking Iraq to Al Qaeda," *New York Times* 12 February 2003 (query.nytimes.com/gst/fullpage.html?res=9D05EEDA163AF931A25751C0A9659C8B63).

20. "White House Publicizes Tape Hours Before Release."

21. "Tape Urges Muslim Fight against U.S."

22. "US Authenticates 'Bin Laden' Tape," BBC News, 15 February 2003 (news.bbc.co.uk/2/hi/middle_east/2765325.stm).

23. For the complete text, see "Bin Laden Tape: Text," BBC News, 12 February 2003 (news.bbc.co.uk/2/hi/middle_east/2751019.stm).

24. William M. Arkin, "When Seeing and Hearing Isn't Believing," *Washington Post* 1 February 1999 (www.washingtonpost.com/wp-srv/national/dotmil/arkin020199.htm).

25. Ibid.

26. Maggie Michael, "Bin Laden, in Statement to U.S. People, Says He Ordered Sept. 11 Attacks," Associated Press, 29 October 2004 (www.signonsandiego.com/news/nation/terror/20041029-1423-binladentape.html).

27. "New Bin Laden Tape Surfaces: Unclear When Tape Was Made," CBS News, 29 October 2004 (cbsnewyork.com/topstories/topstories_story_303162722.html).

28. "The Full Version of Osama bin Laden's Speech [released on October 29, 2004]," Middle East Research Institute, 5 November 2004 (www.memri.org/bin/articles.cgi?Area=sd&ID=SP81104).

29. B. Raman, "OBL's Tape: One More Spin in US Presidential Campaign?" South Asia Analysis Group, 1 November 2004 (www.southasiaanalysis.org/papers12/paper1155.html).

30. Ibid. However, even Raman, in spite of pointing out these problems, accepted the authenticity of the tape, thinking that al-Qaeda used it to influence the American election.

31. "Bin Laden's Warning: Full Text," BBC News, 7 October 2001 (news.bbc.co.uk/2/hi/south_asia/1585636.stm).

32. "BBC Transcript of Osama Bin Laden Statement," 7 November 2001 (news.bbc.co.uk/1/world/monitoring/media_reports/1636782.stm).

33. "Bin Laden's Warning: Full Text."

34. "BBC Transcript of Osama Bin Laden Statement."

35. "Arnaud de Borchgrave Interviews Hameed Gul, Former Chief of Pakistan's Inter Services Intelligence," UPI, 26 September 2001 (www.strategy-page.com/militaryforums/594-499.aspx).

36. See Steve Coll, "Young Osama," *New Yorker* 12 December 2005 (www.newyorker.com/archive/2005/12/12/051212fa_fact), and "In the Footsteps of Bin Laden," CNN, 23 August 2006 (transcripts.cnn.com/TRANSCRIPTS/0608/23/cp.01.html).

37. "In the Footsteps of Bin Laden."

38. "Bin Laden Releases New Videotape," *Larry King Live*, CNN, 29 October 2004 (transcripts.cnn.com/TRANSCRIPTS/0410/29/lkl.01.html).

39. Robert Draper, *Dead Certain: The Presidency of George W. Bush* (New York: Free Press, 2008), 263.

40. Ron Suskind, *The One Percent Doctrine: Deep Inside America's Pursuit of Its Enemies Since 9/11* (New York: Simon & Schuster, 2006), 336.

41. Philip Sherwell, "Bush Takes a Six-Point Lead After New Bin Laden Tape," *Telegraph* 1 November 2004 (www.telegraph.co.uk/news/worldnews/northamerica/usa/1475515/Bush-takes-a-six-point-lead-after-new-bin-Laden-tape.html).

42. "Kerry Blames Defeat on Bin Laden," BBC News, 31 January 2005 (news.bbc.co.uk/2/hi/americas/4222647.stm); "Bush Says Bin Laden Tape Aided Re-Election: Report," Reuters, 28 February 2006 (www.redorbit.com/news/politics/408991/bush_says_bin_laden_tape_aided_reelection_report/).

43. "CIA: New Bin Laden Tape Likely al Qaeda Leader," CNN, 17 December 2004 (www.cnn.com/2004/WORLD/meast/12/16/bin.laden.tape/index.html).

44. "Bin Laden Challenge," *Newshour with Jim Lehrer* transcript, PBS Online Newshour, 16 December 2004 (www.pbs.org/newshour/bb/terrorism/july-dec04/osama_12-16.html).

45. "CIA: New Bin Laden Tape Likely al Qaeda Leader."

46. Ibid.

47. "Timeline: The Search for Bin Laden," BBC News, 23 April 2006 (news.bbc.co.uk/2/hi/south_asia/2827261.stm).

48. See www.middle-east-online.com/english/iraq/?id=12276.

49. "Tape Opposing Iraqi Vote Attributed to bin Laden," Associated Press, 28 December 2004 (www.nytimes.com/2004/12/28/international/middleeast/28laden.html); "'Bin Laden' Calls for Iraqi Poll Boycott," Agence

France-Presse, 28 December 2004 (www.abc.net.au/news/
newsitems/200412/s1272892.htm).

50. Dexter Filkins, "U.S. Says Files Seek Qaeda Aid in Iraq Conflict," *New York Times* 9 February 2004 (query.nytimes.com/gst/
fullpage.html?res=9D00E3D6163AF93AA35751C0A9629C8B63).

51. "In Iraq, a Clear-Cut Bin Laden–Zarqawi Alliance," *Christian Science Monitor* 30 December 2004 (www.csmonitor.com/2004/1230/p01s03-woiq.html).

52. "'Bin Laden' Calls for Iraqi Poll Boycott," Agence France-Presse, 28 December 2004 (www.abc.net.au/news/newsitems/200412/s1272892.htm).

53. "Tape Opposing Iraqi Vote Attributed to bin Laden," Associated Press, 28 December 2004
(www.nytimes.com/2004/12/28/international/middleeast/28laden.html).

54. "U.S. Rejects Bin Laden Tape's 'Truce' Offer," CNN, 19 January 2006
(www.cnn.com/2006/US/01/19/binladen.tape/index.html).

55. Hassan M. Fattah, "Bin Laden Re-emerges, Warning U.S. While Offering 'Truce,'" *New York Times*, 19 January 2006
(www.nytimes.com/2006/01/19/international/middleeast/19cnd-tape.html).

56. "U.S. Rejects Bin Laden Tape's 'Truce' Offer," CNN, 19 January 2006
(www.cnn.com/2006/US/01/19/binladen.tape/index.html).

57. Amber Rupinta, "Duke Professor Skeptical of bin Laden Tape," ABC News, 19 January 2006
(abclocal.go.com/wtvd/story?section=news/local&id=3828678).

58. Tim Weiner, "The Kashmir Connection: A Puzzle," *New York Times* 7 December 2008 (www.nytimes.com/2008/12/07/weekinreview/
07weiner.html).

59. Michael Slackman, "Bin Laden Says West Is Waging War Against Islam," *New York Times* 24 April 2006 (www.nytimes.com/2006/04/24/
world/middleeast/24binladen.html).

60. Ibid.

61. For McClellan's statement, see "Press Gaggle by Scott McClellan," White House, 23 April 2006 (www.whitehouse.gov/news/
releases/2006/04/20060423.html). For an example of a story that simply repeated it, see "White House: US Intel Says Bin Laden Tape Authentic," Reuters, 23 April 2006 (www.boston.com/ news/nation/washington/arti-cles/2006/04/23/white_house_us_intel_says_bin_laden_tape_authentic).

62. "US Believes bin Laden Tape Authentic," Reuters/Australian Broad-casting Corporation News, 24 April 2006
(www.abc.net.au/news/newsitems/200604/s1622041.htm).

63. "On Tape, bin Laden Mourns al-Zarqawi's Death," CNN, 30 June 2006
(edition.cnn.com/2006/WORLD/meast/06/30/ binladen.tape/index.html).

64. "Bin Laden Appears in New al-Qaida Video," Associated Press, 14 July

2007 (www.redorbit.com/news/general/1000484/bin_laden_appears_in_new_
alqaida_video/index.html); Jeffrey Imm, "Newly Released Message: Osama Bin
Laden Calls for Islamic Martyrdom," Counterterrorism Blog, 14 July 2007
(counterterrorismblog.org/2007/07/ osama_bin_laden_july_14.php); Rhonda
Schwartz and Hoda Osman, "Possible New Message from Osama Bin Laden,"
ABC News, 14 July 2007 (blogs.abcnews.com/theblotter/2007/07/possible-
new-me.html).

65. "Bin Laden Slams Global Capitalism in New Video," Associated Press,
6 September 2007 (www.usatoday.com/news/world/2007-09-06-bin-laden-
video_N.htm). The videotape can be seen at alistishhad.wordpress.com/
2007/09/11/as-sahab-shaik-usamah-a-message-to-the-american-people.

66. Brian Ross, "New Videotape From Bin Laden; Al Qaeda's No. 1 Still
Alive," ABC News, 7 September 2007 (blogs.abcnews.com/theblot-
ter/2007/09/new-videotape-f.html).

67. This statement by Ross can be seen in "Coming Soon: New Fake Bin
Laden Video—Just in Time for 9/11," YouTube (www.youtube.com/
watch?v=SZq_4PIbnhI).

68. Ross, "New Videotape from Bin Laden; Al Qaeda's No. 1 Still Alive."
The ABC transcript appeared to have two errors—leaving out "ago" and
having "passed" where Clarke had surely said "pasted."

69. Ibid.

70. "Bin Laden Slams Global Capitalism in New Video."

71. On October 31, 2007, a Fox News segment asking the question,
"Usama Tape Doctored?" interviewed Daveed Gartenstein-Ross, vice president
for research at the Foundation for the Defense of Democracies. When asked
about the beard, he said: "There are only certain circumstances under Islamic
law where you're allowed to dye your beard black. One of those is as a tool of
war, to make yourself seem like a more formidable opponent." Quoted in
David Edwards and Muriel Kane, "Analyst: Still Images Suggest Bin Laden
Video Doctored to Seem New," Raw Story, 1 November 2007
(rawstory.com/news/2007/Osamas_lush_black_beard_in_latest_1101.html).

72. "Ex-CIA Operative Discusses 'The Devil We Know.'"

73. For an example of such ridicule, see "New Osama Bin Laden Video,"
YouTube (www.youtube.com/watch?v=ZEW8pdFuoag). Its bin Laden figure,
with a very long and very black beard, says: "Hello, long time no see. It is me,
Osama bin Laden. And no, this not to be confused with just-for-men hair
color commercial.... I make this video to prove to world that me still alive and
kicking."

74. Robert Windrem and Victor Limjoco, "Was Bin Laden's Last Video
Faked?" MSNBC, 29 October 2007 (www.msnbc.msn.com/id/21530470).

75. Ibid.

76. "Bin Laden Urges Europe to Pull Forces from Afghanistan," Associ-

ated Press, 29 November 2007 (www.cbc.ca/world/story/2007/11/29/
binladen-tape.html).

77. "'Bin Laden Message' to Europeans," BBC News, 29 November 2007
(news.bbc.co.uk/2/hi/south_asia/7119803.stm).

78. "Bin Laden Urges Europe to Pull Forces from Afghanistan."

79. Firouz Sedarat, "Bin Laden Urges Europe to Quit Afghanistan,"
Reuters, 29 November 2007 (uk.reuters.com/article/topNews/
idUKL2912911920071129).

80. "Bin Laden Criticizes EU for Publication of Anti-Islamic Cartoons,"
Associated Press, 20 March 2008 (www.latimes.com/news/ nationworld/
world/la-fg-binladen20mar20,1,7124169.story). An English translation of the
audiotape can be heard at www.reuters.com/resources/ flash/
includevideo.swf?edition=US&videoId=78524.

81. "Purported bin Laden Message: Iraq is 'Perfect Base,'" CNN, 20
March 2008 (www.cnn.com/2008/WORLD/meast/03/19/ binladen.message/
index.html).

82. "'Bin Laden' Message Condemns Israeli Anniversary," *Guardian* 16
May 2008 (www.guardian.co.uk/world/2008/may/16/osamabinladen.alqaida).

83. "Osama Bin Laden Issues New Message," Associated Press, 18 May
2008 (cbs5.com/national/osama.bin.laden.2.726868.html).

84. "Cheney Defends US 'War on Terror,'" Agence France-Presse, 21
December 2008 (www.theage.com.au/world/cheney-defends-us-war-on-terror-
policies-20081222-7345.html).

85. "White House: Bin Laden's Influence Waning," CBS News, 14
January 2009 (www.cbsnews.com/stories/2009/01/14/terror/
main4722301.shtml?source=RSSattr=HOME_4722301).

86. Deb Riechmann, "White House: Audiotape Shows Bin Laden Is
Isolated," Associated Press, 14 January 2009 (www.newsvine.com/_news/
2009/01/14/2309868-white-house-audiotape-shows-bin-laden-is-isolated);
Brian Ross, "Examination of Tape Raises Questions about Osama bin Laden's
Health," ABC News, 15 January 2009 (abcnews.go.com/Blotter/
story?id=6653678&page=1).

87. "Bin Laden Urges War on Israel," BBC, 14 January 2009
(news.bbc.co.uk/2/hi/middle_east/7829716.stm).

88. Deb Riechmann, "White House: Audiotape Shows Bin Laden Is
Isolated."

89. Alan Cowell and Graham Bowley, "Bin Laden, on Tape, Urges Holy
War Over Gaza." This story was originally published in the *New York Times* 15
January 2009, and was available at www.nytimes.com/2009/01/15/world/
middleeast/15mideast.html?_r=1&hp. That URL is now assigned to a different
NYT story, written by Ethan Bronner, and the Cowell–Bowley story is online
at the *International Herald Tribune* ("The Global Edition of the New York

Times"), 14 January 2009 (www.iht.com/articles/2009/01/14/africa/15binladen.php).

90. Brian Ross, "Examination of Tape Raises Questions about Osama bin Laden's Health."

91. Ibid.

92. "Where Is Osama Bin Laden?" CBS News, 7 September 2007 (www.cbsnews.com/stories/2007/09/07/eveningnews/main3243560.shtml).

CHAPTER 4: WHO MIGHT HAVE BEEN MOTIVATED TO FABRICATE MESSAGES?

1. Nick Davies, "How the Spooks Took Over the News," *Independent* 11 February 2008 (www.independent.co.uk/news/media/how-the-spooks-took-over-the-news-780672.html). Davies's *Flat Earth News: An Award-Winning Reporter Exposes Falsehood, Distortion, and Propaganda in the Global Media* was published in 2008 by Random House.

2. Ibid.

3. Dexter Filkins, "U.S. Says Files Seek Qaeda Aid in Iraq Conflict," *New York Times* 9 February 2004 (query.nytimes.com/gst/fullpage.html?res=9D00E3D6163AF93AA35751C0A9629C8B63).

4. Ibid.

5. This fact is criticized in Greg Mitchell, "A U.S. 'Propaganda' Program, al-Zarqawi, and 'The New York Times,'" *Editor and Publisher* 10 April 2006 (editorandpublisher.printthis.clickability.com/pt/cpt?action=cpt&urlID=17866381&partnerID=60).

6. William Safire, "Found, A Smoking Gun," *New York Times* 11 February 2004 (query.nytimes.com/gst/fullpage.html?res=9E06E4DF123AF932A25751C0A9629C8B63).

7. Christopher Dickey, "Shadowland: A (Terrorist's) Letter from Iraq," *Newsweek* 12 February 2004 (www.newsweek.com/id/52981).

8. Rod Nordland, "Is Zarqawi Really the Culprit?" *Newsweek* 6 March 2004 (www.newsweek.com/id/53205).

9. Greg Weiher, "A Purloined Letter: The Zarqawi Gambit," *Counterpunch* 26 February 2004 (www.counterpunch.org/weiher02262004.html).

10. Adrian Blomfield, "How US Fuelled Myth of Zarqawi the Mastermind," *Telegraph* 3 October 2004 (www.telegraph.co.uk/news/worldnews/middleeast/iraq/1473309/How-US-fuelled-myth-of-Zarqawi-the-mastermind.html).

11. Thomas E. Ricks, "Military Plays Up Role of Zarqawi," *Washington Post* 10 April 2006 (www.washingtonpost.com/wp-dyn/content/article/2006/04/09/AR2006040900890_pf.html).

12. Chris Tomlinson, "Impact: Pentagon Ups Public Relations Spending," Associated Press, 5 February 2009 (www.startribune.com/nation/39161127.html).

13. Ricks, "Military Plays Up Role of Zarqawi."

14. Quoted in Davies, "How the Spooks Took Over the News."

15. William M. Arkin, "When Seeing and Hearing Isn't Believing," *Washington Post* 1 February 1999 (www.washingtonpost.com/wp-srv/national/dotmil/arkin020199.htm).

16 John Hanna, "AP CEO: Bush Turned Military Into Propaganda Machine," Huffington Post, 9 February 2009 (www.huffingtonpost.com/2009/02/06/ap-ceo-bush-turned-milita_n_164812.html).

17 Tomlinson, "Impact: Pentagon Ups Public Relations Spending."

CHAPTER 5: THE CONVENIENT TIMING OF MANY OF THE MESSAGES

1. Walter Pincus and Karen DeYoung, "U.S. Says New Tape Points to Bin Laden," *Washington Post* 9 December 2001 (www.washingtonpost.com/wp-dyn/content/article/2007/11/18/AR2007111800690.html).

2. Brian Whitaker, "Bin Laden Voice on Video, Says TV Channel," *Guardian* 10 September 2002 (www.guardian.co.uk/media/2002/sep/10/alqaida.september112001).

3. Ibid.

4. "Al Jazeera: Bin Laden Tape Praises Hijackers," CNN, 9 September 2001 (archives.cnn.com/2002/WORLD/meast/09/09/binladen.tape).

5. Jason Burke, "Bin Laden Still Alive, Reveals Spy Satellite," *Guardian* 6 October 2002 (www.guardian.co.uk/world/2002/oct/06/alqaida.terrorism).

6. James Risen, "Qaeda Broadcast; Experts Conclude That Voice on Tape Belongs to bin Laden," *New York Times* 19 November 2002 (query.nytimes.com/gst/fullpage.html?res=9D05E1DD1E30F93AA25752C1A9649C8B63).

7. "Purported bin Laden Message on War against Infidels," CNN, 12 February 2003 (www.cnn.com/2003/WORLD/meast/02/11/ binladen.excerpts).

8. Ron Suskind, *The One Percent Doctrine: Deep Inside America's Pursuit of Its Enemies Since 9/11* (New York: Simon & Schuster, 2006), 336.

9. Hassan M. Fattah, "Qaeda Deputy Taunts Bush for 'Failure' in Airstrike," *New York Times* 31 January 2006 (query.nytimes.com/gst/fullpage.html?res=9C07E1D91E3FF932A05752C0A9609C8B63).

10. William Kates, "Study: Terror Warnings Up Approval Ratings," Associated Press, 26 October 2004 (www.informationclearinghouse.info/article7152.htm).

11. "Bin Laden Dismisses Moussaoui 9/11 Role," Associated Press, 24 May 2006 (www.washingtontimes.com/news/2006/may/23/20060523-111941-6924r).

12. Rebecca Wittman, "RE: Results from Nationwide Poll, Zogby America, 5/12/06 through 5/16/06," 911Truth.org (www.911truth.org/page.php?page=zogby_2006).

13. "Time's Up on Escalation," Think Progress, 10 July 2007 (thinkprogress.org/escalation-list).

14. Ibid.; Noam N. Levey, "Republican Discord on Iraq Grows: Once Staunch Allies, More GOP Lawmakers Are Dissenting from the Administration, Urging a Change of Course," *Los Angeles Times* 7 July 2007 (articles.latimes.com/2007/jul/07/nation/na-warvote7); Ron Brynaert, "Two More GOP Senators Break from Bush on Iraq," Raw Story, 8 July 2007 (rawstory.com/news/2007/Two_more_GOP_senators_break_from_0707.html).

15. "Bin Laden Appears in New al-Qaida Video," Associated Press, 14 July 2007 (www.breitbart.com/article.php?id=D8QCMG080&show_article=1); "Al Qaeda Releases New Recording," ABC News, 14 December 2007 (blogs.abcnews.com/theblotter/2007/12/alleged-al-qaed.html).

16. "Bin Laden Slams Global Capitalism in New Video," Associated Press, 8 September 2007 (www.usatoday.com/news/world/2007-09-06-bin-laden-video_N.htm).

17. "Zogby Poll: 51% of Americans Want Congress to Probe Bush/Cheney Regarding 9/11 Attacks," Zogby International, 6 September 2007 (www.zogby.com/news/ReadNews.cfm?ID=1354).

18. E-mail letter, 8 January 2009.

SUMMARY AND CONCLUSION

1. Quoted in Robert Windrem, "Where is Osama Bin Laden? An Analysis," Deep Background, NBC, 13 June 2008 (deepbackground.msnbc.msn.com/archive/2008/06/13/1138296.aspx). In spite of this fact, however, the assurances from reporters and experts kept coming. As we saw earlier, former CIA analyst Michael Scheuer assured us in 2004 that bin Laden was "certainly on the border somewhere between Pakistan and Afghanistan," while Richard Clarke said in 2007 that he was most likely in Southeast Asia. In August 2008, *New York Times* reporter Eric Lichtblau assured us that "Osama bin Laden [is] still at large" ("Bush Seeks to Affirm a Continuing War on Terror," *New York Times* 29 August 2008 [www.nytimes.com/2008/08/30/washington/30terror.html?partner=rssuserland &emc=rss&pagewanted=all]). In a report on the seventh anniversary of 9/11, CBS News said: "Seven years after Sept. 11, 2001, ... the mastermind of the deadliest terrorist attacks on American soil, Osama bin Laden, is still at large and leading a resurgent al Qaeda" ("7 Years Later, No Closer To Bin Laden," CBS News, 11 September 2008 [www.cbsnews.com/stories/2008/09/11/earlyshow/main4438342.shtml]).

2. "Ex-CIA Operative Discusses 'The Devil We Know,'" Interview with Terry Gross on *Fresh Air*, WHYY, 2 October 2008 (www.npr.org/templates/story/story.php?storyId=95285396).

INDEX